Taking Cues from Kids

TAKING CUES FROM KIDS

HOW THEY THINK

∞

WHAT TO DO ABOUT IT

DOROTHY PETERS

Foreword by
DEBORAH MEIER

HEINEMANN
PORTSMOUTH, NH

Heinemann
A division of Reed Elsevier Inc.
361 Hanover Street
Portsmouth, NH 03801–3912
www.heinemann.com

Offices and agents throughout the world

0-325-00210-X

Library of Congress Cataloging-in-Publication Data
CIP data on file at the Library of Congress.

Editor: Lois Bridges
Production: Merrill Peterson, Matrix Productions
Cover design: Jenny Jensen Greenleaf
Cover and interior photographs: Nancy Sirkis
Manufacturing: Louise Richardson

Printed in the United States of America on acid-free paper
Docutech RRD 2004

To my colleagues at Central Park East School who, in the earlier years, informed my practice, and who, today, help my student teachers inform theirs.

To those who read the manuscript and whose Post-Its shaped its several versions.

- *Kristine Annunziato and Nicole Gadek, former student teachers, now teachers*
- *Karen Cathers, teacher*
- *Donna Lipmann, resource room teacher*
- *Judy Mage, social worker*
- *Georgia Wever, parent*

To Nancy Sirkis, for photographs.

To Mary Williams, who converted the first manuscript from my typewriter to the computer and rescued all subsequent drafts from my inexperienced computer fingers.

To Dr. Frances Schoonmaker, whose suggestions helped turn the manuscript into a book.

To Jane Andreas, CPE director, who always makes me welcome and who, with her staff, arranged for photo taking, releases, and interviews.

To Debbie Meier, who critiqued the book and brought me to CPE.

And especially to my friend, knowledgeable and thoughtful teacher Hettie Jordan-Villanova, who critiqued all drafts, suggested layouts, provided ideas, and confirmed my purpose.

Finally, to the student teachers whose insightful questions and deep doubts forced me to refine my thinking and find the words to explain my teaching more precisely.

Contents

∞

Foreword

The life of schoolchildren is made up of very particular details. So, too, is their teacher's. It is in these interactions—what David Hawkins called the "I, thou, and it"—that learning occurs. It's always, in the end, a "you" and a "me" fascinated by an "it." And it is this essential relationship between people—child to child, child to teacher—that underlies Dottie Peter's remarkable book. Imagine what it is like to be in the presence of teachers such as those you meet in these pages, day in and day out. It is in the detailed conversations that would-be teachers have with Dottie and with children in their new classrooms that the most powerful lifelong learning occurs. In the end it's the company we keep—and that includes other children and other adults—that determines the quality of our schooling.

The "I, thou, and it" principle remains true in schools even though schools, unlike other more natural forms of apprenticeship learning, are so overwhelmingly involved in issues of management. The business of schooling often overwhelms the business of learning. Schoolkeeping is not an evil, an invention of bureaucrats, but just the humdrum backdrop that even in the best of all worlds demands attention.

Keeping the two—learning and management—in balance is hard to do in modern schools. And many teachers and many schools are undone by the effort. We've spawned a huge industry that's largely devoted to the "business of schooling" and, consequently, we may spend less and less time on what's going on down there between kids and teachers.

So it's extraordinarily helpful to have this series of letters by my friend and erstwhile colleague to a group of student teachers who are struggling to make sense of and internalize this balance. Dottie helps these dozen student teachers, in elementary school classrooms in schools I know well, to make sense of what they see—both the chaos and the order, as she puts it—and find their own possible place within it. Throughout, she strives to help the student teachers focus on the "I, thou, and it." She helps them avoid the twin evils of rigidity and planlessness.

The classrooms described in this book are often messy and always vigorous, a necessary condition when one is committed to following children's interests. Children's ways of learning with glue and paint and cardboard are not neat. Following children's own "wonderful" ideas may mean deviating from pre-scribed curriculum, another source of student-teacher anxiety. Yet does not a democratic social order require citizens who see themselves as active agents and participants, and is there not a connection between that requirement and these classrooms with their active, decision-making children?

Where our capacity to exercise judgment in the classroom is stifled in the name of consistency and order, so, too is our vision of democracy narrowed with its similar messy and unpredictable ups and downs, its seeming waste of time, its inefficiencies. Learning to tolerate the "waste of time" that democracy requires is part of the task of good schooling. Truly hearing each other takes time. When we can't afford the time, teachers and parents get cut off from a direct and powerful voice in the education of the young. Silenced adults don't make good company for children learning to become good citizens.

Dottie doesn't insist that her student teachers agree with what they see, but she demands that they try to understand it. In doing so, I learned a lot myself about schools I thought I knew well, and about practices I had a lot to do with introducing, promoting, and supporting. It helped me, as I read this work, to think about ways in which I too have changed my viewpoint and practices since I founded the Central Park East schools nearly thirty years ago. I longed again for a time when I could imagine each teacher building his or her work on each child's own interests, without regard for city or state frameworks. Dottie reminds me of how confident I once was that the best environment for children was not overly dependent on adults who could step in quickly to resolve, extend, and direct children. The care-ful attention to space (so that children can function independently of the teacher) that begins the first letters to Nicky and Lisa was startling to me.

I've grown accustomed to forgetting it. But in fact it's as true today as it was thirty years ago.

I've taken it for granted, and yet also forgotten.

These letters remind me of why I like being back in a schoolhouse again after several years of focus on trying to produce large-scale reform, systemic this and that, through my work with the Annenberg Institute for School Reform. The larger society of experts often loses track of the relationship between our big ideas and how they appear in the daily lives of teachers, parents, and children. Of course. After all, teachers do it too—right there in the midst of school. They start off with large ideas and are often stymied turning these ideas into practices that work for a specific group of kids. Dottie reminds us that wisdom is cumulative and the experiences of other teachers and other schools, as well as research on teaching and learning, are critical experiences to take with us into our classrooms.

In too much of the world, the uniqueness of each child and each classroom is acknowledged, then papered over with grand frameworks, assessments, curricular scripts, and pressure for ever more grandiose coverage of subject matter and skills. It's amazing how hard it is for folks determined to change the whole world fast to remember the damage they do when they ignore the particularities that this book is about. No grand design can eliminate our idiosyncratic responses to the world. But some policies can lessen their power and importance, can cut them off close to their roots and leave us more alienated, more rootless. In the hands of a strong administration, consistent policies, and unrelenting accountability it can appear possible to operate a school that barely notices all those ornery kids, their different actual understandings, the unique adaptations they make to the world the school presents to them, their habits of heart, mind, and work that are the real outcomes of schooling. But for adults to whom these things are the fundamentals of schooling, Dottie's letters offer powerful evidence and powerful lessons for practice—including the practice of making policy.

Deborah Meier
Founding Director, Central Park East Schools, New York City
Principal, Mission Hill School, Boston

Preface

When I was six, I attended the Rudolf Steiner School in New York City. I remember virtually nothing about being six. But I do remember learning to add and subtract by pushing acorn cups into different piles on my desk. Something about the feel of those acorn cups and the aesthetics of the shape of them stays with me nearly three-quarters of a century later.

The next year, when I was seven, the Depression struck. My father lost his business. We moved out of New York City. I went to public school. In that school our desks were in rows; we were seated alphabetically. Since my last name started with "Z," I had the last seat in the last row. I was the smallest child in the class. Never mind that I could not see the blackboard on which the teacher wrote our lessons. That year I learned to run with the boys on my block, to climb trees, and to play hooky from school.

A year later, when I was eight, my father began to earn a living again. We moved back to the city, and I was enrolled in the Lincoln School of Teachers College, a "John Dewey" school. My memories of those years include our turning our desks on their sides to create a cave when we studied primitive man. I sewed a fake fur costume as a member of the clothing committee. I remember hammering the outer stalk of a flax plant to get at the silky fibers inside, which we would spin into thread as part of a study of Colonial America. In high school I planted seedlings on the side of a hill to prevent erosion, part of a study of farm life. I remember a study of Harlem—of poverty, segregation, churches, music. This curriculum arose from an event in our own lives—the stoning of us white kids by black kids as we walked from the subway through their neighborhood to our all-white school.

Of my college learning, with its textbooks and professorial lectures, I remember virtually nothing.

So it was natural that when, several careers and many years later, I decided to become a teacher, it should be to teach in a classroom that would be a children's workshop, noisy with the sound of hammers and colorful with the splatter of paint. I wanted a classroom that would engage the child's total energy—of mind, body, emotions. It needed to be a classroom for the lover of words, and also for the artist, the builder, the mechanic, and the dreamer.

That Southside Chicago neighborhood where I began my teaching was our laboratory. We collected seeds from the honey locusts, hazarded guesses as to how many might grow, and planted them in window boxes. We brought clumps of frozen earth from the vacant lot and thawed them in a fish bowl to see if anything survived in the winter ground. We visited the lake, the park, the train track, the building site where new housing began to rise. We went behind the meat counter at the local butcher's and then visited the city's wholesale market to view the sides of meat hanging from hooks.

In the classroom we built our own structures, made our own lake in a tub, cooked, and wrote about our discoveries.

It was energetic, loud, and messy. There was so much I didn't know. How to keep the joy and spontaneity and yet maintain an acceptable decibel level. How to keep the pattern blocks and rods from their everyday jumble together. How to keep track of who learned what when six or eight activities ran simultaneously. How to choose which experiences should follow which. Did they need to build on one another in some organized way, or was a wide scattering of experiences just as good? And how to balance the things that seemed educationally valid to me with the need for required basal readers and Mastery Learning.

My principal was supportive but didn't know the "how-to" of learner-centered education. Colleagues varied from being mildly interested to openly hostile. The next nine years were fun, but they were lonely.

Then a lucky break. In 1982, Debbie Meier opened her second alternative public school in East Harlem.[1] When part of the staff from Central Park East 1 (CPE 1) moved to CPE 2, there was room for me at CPE 1. For ten years I was surrounded by energetic, enthusiastic colleagues. The atmosphere was full of questions asked, ideas shared, the pros and cons of everything, respect for each other and support for risk taking. The ragged strands of my teaching knit more firmly together; the pattern became more coherent.

When I became a supervisor of student teachers of the Preservice Program of Teachers College, Columbia University, it seemed crucial to me that these young teachers experience this vibrant form of education. Most of my student teachers were placed at CPE 1 and CPE 2. The placement in learner-centered classrooms was culture shock. What they saw was so different from their own educational experience. Even though most of them had philosophically decided on child-centeredness, they needed help in understanding what they saw and how to accomplish it.

Intelligent, perceptive, constructively critical, these student teachers raised issues that all educational practitioners committed to child-centered

approaches need to consider. They asked important "how-to" questions—
how to individualize instruction in a group of thirty, how to work from
children's ideas and questions and be sure that in so doing children would
learn what they needed to know, how to balance choice and teacher authority, how to keep kids "on task," how to know whether learning has taken
place. We met weekly to discuss these issues. The student teachers kept
reflective journals to which I wrote responses, and we discussed further.

All of us who work in classrooms know that there is no such thing as a
homogeneous classroom. Even within the most rigorously tracked school,
each classroom is made up of unique individuals—children who move
faster or slower along the prescribed track, children who learn in different
and idiosyncratic ways. Sometimes we spark the energy of the child to connect him to learning. Sometimes we fail.

We know also that modern theories of development postulate the exist-
ence of multiple intelligences.[2] To help each child achieve her full potential,
we have to focus our lens on the child as individual—to see her as an individual thinker, as artist, as architect, as mechanic, as athlete. When we focus
our lens this way, we may then see how to provide the multiple pathways to
learning that children need. If we do that, we may reach them all.

But how do we learn to do that? Individualized instruction and the provision of multiple pathways to learning have a long tradition.[3] A small number
of schools operating within the progressive education or learner-centered
classroom model exist; these might serve as models.[4] Further, a growing
number of teachers within traditional schools have created "constructivist"
classrooms, communities of learners, where children take responsibility for
their own learning and for that of the community. These teachers actively
encourage individual responses to literature and writing. Within their print
learning curriculum, they focus the lens on the individual child.

Sharpening this lens and expanding its use across the curriculum is not
easy. One has to overcome one's own education, perhaps, where teacher
was the provider of information, and the student the memorizer of correct
answers. The moves for mandated curriculum and uniform standards—
whatever their merit—tend to push thinking further away from the creation
of diverse approaches to meet the different needs of different children. Colleagues to share one's concerns, one's self-doubts, who will support one's
efforts to deepen and sharpen one's skills, are sometimes hard to find.

One needs constantly to revisit the thinking and daily practices that the lens
requires, to hear the voices of those who try to look closely at children. As we
change what we do, we need to see that we are not alone, that others share our

questions and our self-doubts. We need to see the same tentative steps we take others take also. To hold our focus, we need to be supported and affirmed.

The story of this book is the story of the growth of a group of student teachers as reflected through their journal entries and my responses. Their struggle and their growth were not different from our own. Their questions and their successes are ours as well. It is my hope that as you read about their year, you will recognize your own victories, celebrate them, and find yourself affirmed.

HOW TO READ THIS BOOK

The material in this book could have been sorted into subject matter chapters. Instead, the dialogue is presented pretty much as it occurred. For us, discipline came up early on and reappeared throughout the year. So did everything else. Dealing with different children on different days in seemingly different situations brought us back over and over to basic ideas and firmed our understanding of how to apply these ideas in daily practice. Learning takes place through multiple, partial experiences, in concrete situations, over time. Therefore, the journal form seemed appropriate. (For those who prefer the subject matter approach, an index is supplied.)

Each chapter contains three components:

1. Quotes from student teachers—taken from their journal queries, observations, and comments—that frame the chapter discussion
2. Bulleted list of the primary topics the chapter addresses
3. Responses I wrote to student teachers

The material evolves in a chronological manner. At the beginning, we explore issues that reflect the start of a new year and continue our exploration to the final months and graduation. Near the end of the book, in Chapter 11, four teachers in different schools suggest ways to begin. The appendices offer ideas for setting up the room, organizing the day, where to scrounge for materials. Tracy Kramer's "lesson plan for an individual child" is an example of how to plan instruction for one child. A list of suggested readings completes the book.

All names in the book are pseudonyms. Where several student teachers of like personality teaching the same age group raised identical questions, I used the question and response that seemed best to explain. Student teachers Ellen, Johnisha, Nicky, Patrick, and Tamara taught in pre-K through second grades. Student teachers Sam, Martha, and Rebecca taught in third/fourth grades; student teachers Lisa, Vera, and Beth taught in fifth/sixth grades.

Introduction

∞

Three major beliefs underlie learner-centered classroom teaching. These beliefs are:

1. Children build knowledge out of their own experiencing.
2. Teaching should be and can be individualized.
3. The teacher is less a provider of answers and more a poser of questions that the child may wish to investigate.

The day in a learner-centered classroom often starts with morning meeting (although some teachers opt for quiet reading first and meeting later). Meeting is the time when the day is organized and children make their work choices. The day's calendar is reviewed; a whole-class short discussion or minilesson may take place. With older children, when projects are ongoing, the teacher checks the child's plan for the day. Or the teacher may skip this meeting altogether, just checking at the door that each child has his or her morning plan in mind.

Project or work time follows. This is the time when "curriculum" is happening. The class may be studying a single subject—the neighborhood, water, the Maya, explorers (each child studying that piece which interests him or her)—or there may be no overall science/social studies theme, each child picking for investigation a topic of particular importance to him or her.

Invariably, a large number of activities go on simultaneously: painting, model making in foamboard, papier-maché, or "junk" materials; cooking, sewing, experiments with a variety of common substances, library research, and, more typically (but not exclusively) in the lower grades, sand and water tables, block building, animal and plant observations, and dress-up dramatic play.

The teacher circulates between work tables and areas, assessing the children's product and process, making comments and asking the questions he or she anticipates will push observation, hypothesis making, further inquiry, and deeper learning. There are few whole-class lessons, little "up front" teaching.

Morning and afternoon, even during quiet reading and writing times, the visitor is aware of children coming and going on their own—to chorus, recorder, violin, or other out-of-class activity. The day flows from one activity to another. There are no 45-minute bells.

How to look at such a day? How to understand it? How to tell if "order" exists behind "chaos"? That's where my student teachers and I began.

Taking Cues from Kids

CHAPTER 1

Beginnings: Is It Chaos?
Looking for Structure

∞

I was surprised when I entered the classroom. I did not see any desks. Instead, there were tables and rugs set up in different areas of the room. It is so different from my elementary school experience with its rows of desks and textbooks. I will be interested to see how my teacher maintains control over the students . . .

Johnisha

Where are the students' desks and chairs? Where is the Teacher's Big Desk? There is no definite front of the room. I feel a little disoriented . . .

Martha

My teacher says much can be learned from chaos . . .

Rebecca

At 10:15 the Ks arrived. Suddenly the room felt very chaotic. Sam was clinging to his mother for dear life. Charlie was crying, as was Allie. Today Jordana was the only child crying and clinging to her mother. My teacher partnered her with Emily, a first grader, but Jordana's crying soon caused Emily to become upset so that both were crying . . .

Ellen

∞ Looking for structure

∞ *Room Layout*—an environment for independence

∞ Materials that teach

∞ Simultaneous activities

- Teacher freed for individualized teaching
- *Organization of the day*—Morning meeting
- Routines
- Choice chart
- Day's calendar
- *Rules*
- Desirable behaviors acknowledged
- Crying disease
- Parents in the classroom
- Stepping back from helping
- Practicing conflict resolution
- Whole group vs. small group, appropriateness of each
- Beware of silence

Dear Rebecca,

Thanks for sharing with me your ambivalence about learner-centered education. What an excellent way for us to begin! You have concerns about the "sort of chaotic creative environment" you see and your lack of confidence about starting out yourself with "things slightly or more than slightly out of control." These are important concerns shared by many teachers who would like to change what they do but are afraid of "control" issues. Yes, that can be a scary feeling.

We need to deal with "chaos" at our lunch meeting—how to prevent it and to what extent it's our perception that there's chaos and that things are out of control. Although they may be; it does happen even in the best of learner-centered classrooms.

I've asked each of you to look for the structures that make the room work. I think you will find that learner-centered classrooms are not less structured than traditional ones, but are differently structured. When you see that structures are there and that the teacher has created them, I think that the room will seem less chaotic and more under control. Knowing that the teacher has control, you will feel more confident that you too can teach successfully this way, should you choose to do so.

But let's take a look.

Let's begin with physical structure—the room layout.

What are some of the things the teacher has thought about in arranging the room as she has? Looking at the room can you tell something about the teacher's ideas of how children learn and what she thinks they should learn. In particular, where has she placed the responsibility for learning? How can you tell? Also look at the supplies the teacher has put out. Why has the teacher put out what he/she has? That is, one teacher may have put out sewing materials, another not. Is it personal preference? Is there a learning or management issue involved? Are there materials that can be used only in one way? Many ways? Advantages/disadvantages of each? Bring your observations and a sketch of the room to lunch and we'll share the analysis.

Dottie

∞

Dear Nicky,

Thank you for sharing your room analysis with us. You really noticed a lot!

The low furniture so that the teacher can see everywhere and be aware of what kids are doing—even when lots of different things are going on simultaneously. The tall bookcase you perhaps can't help. You don't always get your choice of furniture! But if the principal is willing, you might cut it in half and set the shelves back-to-back so you still have an area divider—one you could see over. If she's not willing, you'll have to remember to walk over there once in awhile . . . especially if there's suddenly a lot of noise.

Second, you noticed the tables grouped in small clusters, to encourage conversation and group work but to discourage large and noisy get-togethers.

The shelves labeled, with corresponding labels on the equipment—"pencils go here," "chapter books," etc.

Shelves for work-in-progress. Shelf tops for special displays.

Clean-up stuff—sponges, brooms, dustpans.

Traffic patterns. Kids can move between areas and around the room without knocking into each other or each other's work. Messy work, like painting, away from the library area where so many books are, and near the sink, for easy clean-up. Nothing like a trail of spilled water or a river of paint across the room to ruin your day!

Multiuse of space. Bookshelves and supply shelves as storage and as area dividers. And finally, the whole-class meeting area used as a place for the whole community to gather as well as a work space other times.

The teacher's role was to design an environment that kids can use largely without her direction—an environment that says to kids, "You can learn on your own. You know where things are when you need them. You know where they go when it's time to clean up. You don't need me to give you each sheet of paper. You can do it by yourself."

Dottie

᳁

Dear Lisa,

The upper grade rooms do look different from the lower grades. You don't necessarily see areas for sand and water, for blocks—although you might from time to time during the year. But, as you realized, the principle is the same. The room is organized into sensible areas where supplies and equipment can be found—and returned—by the kids. Stuff is still labeled; science stuff in one area, math in another, art and construction stuff in another. There are shelves for work-in-progress and for display. Cleaning supplies are on hand. Table grouping, traffic patterns for these larger people have been considered. There's a meeting area. As in the lower grades, a classroom has been created that the children can use largely independently of the teacher. "You know where the stuff is. You can figure out what you need for your work. The responsibility lies with you."

By the way, wasn't that a nice labeling of shelves and areas Ellen described for the K-1 room? "This is the block area. Five children may work here"—words and drawings to show the five kids. And on the shelves an outline of the size block that goes there—a daily activity of matching size and shape that also contributes to order!

Color coding helps with the book organization, doesn't it? And while your older kids only need a written recipe for cooking and written shelf labels, these little ones have words and pictures to show where to put measuring cups and spoons, bowls, and flour. Informal reading made easy!

Additionally, the setting up of an environment that the kids can use with minimal teacher help, filled with materials that in themselves teach, makes it possible to have many activities going simultaneously and frees you, the teacher, to facilitate the learning for different children in different ways. Individualized teaching becomes possible.

More on that later!

So the first structure in a learner-centered classroom is a room plan that makes it physically possible for children to work largely on their own, independently of the teacher.

Dottie

P.S. A suggestion for hand washing in a room without a sink. Your kids do handle cleaning up in the bathroom quite well, but you might want to set up a gallon of water next to a small hand basin, on a tray. Cut paper towels in half, put them in a small container, also soap in its own container. And a wastebasket right there. Two kids can wash hands at the same time, each pouring the water for the other. Saves trips out of the room.

∽

Dear Nicky,

We're ready to look at the *second structure. The organization of the day.*
    Here are the questions for each of you.
    How does your teacher organize the day? What does morning meeting contribute to structure? How do the kids know what to do? Are there routines? Do they provide structure? How? The choice chart? The day's calendar?
    We'll share at lunch.

Dottie

∽

Dear Rebecca,

Thanks for sharing the organization of the day in your room. Yes, your teacher has figured out how each part should go, from the hanging up of coats, to the returning of borrowed books, to the quiet way of coming to the meeting area with a book to look at while the teacher does the morning check-ins. And the kids know exactly what to do, don't they? Nice that the teacher acknowledges how well they do each day. That positive reinforcement really is part of her "structure," isn't it?
    You note that a couple of kids have problems sitting still during meeting while the schedule and work sign-up is going on. You might, as teacher, want to prepare ahead of time for this. Where it's the same kids each day,

you may want to seat them next to you so you can pat or stroke them to quiet them when they get antsy.

Older kids may not want to be patted, but the idea of strategic seating—before an incident occurs—still applies.

So morning meeting organizes the day, the choice chart where you put their names as they make choices for work helps them remember what to do, the 5-minute warning to finish up the work eases the transitions, and the posted schedule reinforces the "What comes next?" piece of it. The routines remain fairly consistent day to day to maintain a sense of security. Kids, particularly little ones, need the security that comes when they can predict "what's going to happen next." I remember once a little one asking, "Teacher, have we had lunch yet?" Lunch is such a good marker for the day!

The room structure you will set up before school starts in the fall. The structure of the day you will also decide in advance (but note, neither is written in stone; you may want to change them later on.) And now come *the rules that are the third part of a learner-centered classroom structure*. What are the rules? Where did they come from? Are desirable behaviors acknowledged—over and over again—so as to be rewarded and to set a tone for the room?

Are there consequences for rule infringement? How does the teacher deal with behaviors?

Might it be different for different kids? So take a look and we'll share at lunch.

Dottie

∞

Dear Nicky,

Yes, you have to set rules early on and reinforce them forever. Definitely begin the first day of school. You have two options—set the rules yourself or do it with the kids. Rules should be few and simple.

At CPE they fall under RESPECT.

- We respect each other's person. Therefore, we don't fight.
- We respect each other's feelings. We don't call names.
- We respect each other's work. We don't mess it up. (Maybe this happens more with little kids?)

A teacher I know has a simple rule: *Every person has a right to learn and to feel safe*; no one has a right to interfere with others' learning or feeling safe.

I always add my own fourth rule. "We work with quiet, inside voices."

If you decide to set the rules with the kids, you might set forth these three areas of respect or state the "learning and safety rule" and ask kids what kinds of behaviors and actions might promote the rule. Try for some positive "We do" behaviors. Kids, like teachers, tend to think of the "don'ts" more easily, which leaves them without ideas for acceptable alternative behaviors! We *do* say, "I could help you with that." We *do* say, "We could share the scissors," and so on.

I wouldn't make a long written list of rules. Instead, make it a thoughtful discussion, probably fairly short, so that behavior doesn't look like a thing you're worried about, but a thing you are confident they'll be able to manage.

You'll also want to discuss with them the way they think clean up should go. Should each person clean up his own mess? Should everyone work until all the clean up is done? What should they do when they're finished?

Then you need lots of praise, acknowledgment of the good behaviors you see. "I noticed today how well you listened to each other in discussion. I noticed Thomas picked up all the dropped rods, and Elwin helped Sasha with the paints. Good for you."

I've even stopped the whole class to say "Sorry I interrupted your work, but I just saw a wonderful thing." And then I'd describe the wonderful behavior.

I think also that a quiet teacher voice and quiet signals (like lights off for quiet) contribute to quiet ways with the kids.

No arguments either about infringement of rules in group meeting. "Please raise your hand." "Hold on, So-and-so, we need more people listening before you go on."

A silent shake of your head will silence some kids. Insist on people sitting out of the meeting if they can't handle it. And, of course, if you know that some kids always have trouble, use preventative measures. Sit them next to you, or away from their friends. These are quiet ways. I think they will work for you.

Dottie

∞

Dear Rebecca,

Do talk with the teacher about the structures related to work standards. Maybe the kids can do any project they want? I doubt it. Can they drop their project at any time? I doubt that, too. What about the quality of the work? Can they do any old sloppy thing? How does the teacher establish a standard of acceptability? If these are negotiable issues, that in itself is a structure. What are the bases for the negotiation?

Re Paul and his indecisiveness. This may be an instance where a teacher needs to be more directive for the child's own good. He may be a child who can be given a chance to make a choice about what to work on, but may have to have his options narrowed. "You may do this or this." He may not be able to make a choice easily. Is he afraid to risk? Making a choice is making a commitment to work, isn't it? Is he afraid he can't work successfully? What kind of teacher supports do you think he needs?

Dottie

∽

Dear Ellen,

You write so well. I laughed so at the "crying disease."

Crying disease shows you the children are getting comfortable at school. They're over the first days' fear when they held it all in to be "good." Now they feel safe, so they let it all out. Not to worry; a pat and then sending them off to work keeps the whole thing in proportion for them.

Parents in the classroom. A good idea. As you recognize, school is a big experience for little kids: their first time away from home. The classroom is an enormous new world. It helps to have mama there. As teacher, welcome and introduce the mamas to the whole class. Invite them to look around, ask them to help put on the kids' name tags or whatever else would be useful, or ask them to sit quietly at the edge so their kids can be part of the class.

Ask them to stay until their kid seems comfortable and remind them to say good-bye before they leave, not to just disappear. Those without mamas present who need one will use you or maybe share a mama.

Once in awhile, you'll have to wean a parent. It may be her anxiety, not the kid's, you're dealing with. "Oh, Ms. So-and-so, Jeannie is doing so well for the first day of school, I think she doesn't need you to stay today."

You ask if Carol should be in kindergarten instead of in first grade. I really don't know. There are many factors to consider in deciding a child's placement: most importantly, her physical size and social development. Where will she be comfortable? A learner-centered classroom teacher is focused on assessing each child's need and providing for that individual child. So it ought not to be an issue if academically she still needs what we might consider kindergarten-level work. Not all kids move at the same speed; no big deal. A first-grade room has lots of stuff that can be used at many levels . Note the differences in complexity of building that occurs in the block area, for example. And lots of opportunity when kids work together for them to fertilize each other and "teach" each other how to do things.

There are lots of reading opportunities, too, as you notice. All the shelves are labeled with pictures and words so that kids can read where to put things. The class schedule is up. The kids' names are posted . Pictures they've drawn and words about those pictures are on the walls, and you'll notice at reading time that kids read together, or can listen to a book on tape while they follow the print, and that the teacher gives individual help according to what he sees kids need. Not a big deal to have a wide spectrum of abilities in a room where the teacher knows how to manage individualized instruction.

Dottie

∞

Dear Lisa,

Good for you. You saw you could have kids help each other choose books instead of your having to help each child! Good for you. Make yourself a rule and repeat it to yourself each time a kid asks you for help. (1) Is this a thing he could do for himself or figure out for himself? (2) Is there another kid or a resource he could think of that might help him? (3) If neither of the above, then, and only then, will I help.

Example: You're going to the library with Lara to find a book on amphibians. Could she have gone to the library by herself? Could she have asked the librarian to show her where to look? Maybe your "teacher" role at this point was to help her think out how she could accomplish this task without you.

Are there several children who could benefit from a minilesson on library skills at this point? This would be a better use of your teacher time than to accompany Lara.

You also caught the problem of whether you should type for the kids. Maybe the decision should be whether they should type the report at all, if they can't do it themselves. Maybe they should take turns typing, while the nontypist does some other work, rather than having the nontypist sitting and watching. You have to weigh your time availability, the most productive use of your time, and what the kids learn/don't learn if you do the work for them. Of course, the finished product will look nicer if you type it, but what have the kids learned? I'm not saying don't do it; I'm suggesting some of the things to think about.

I'm glad you had a chance to revisit the violence issue. It's important that the children know how you feel about it. Unlikely, by itself, to change much, however. Kids need to practice conflict resolution as real conflicts arise in the classroom and school—more than once.

Also point out the examples when appropriate. Do our teachers fight with each other? Call each other names? How do they resolve their differences? You could even make a social studies unit out of it! I'm not suggesting you do, but you could. Look at the violence in society, look at the methods of nonviolence; Gandhi, Martin Luther King, demonstrations, boycotts, etc. Could be a very rich study.

Re the whole-group activities not going as well: Large groups are hard to do under any circumstances.

You write that you wished the class would have been silent while you presented your lesson. Yes, good manners are important—required, in fact. Part of it is what you choose to do with the whole class. Some things are best taught one on one, some in small groups, some whole class. You need to think which format will work most effectively for each of your activities. And then you have to establish the structures for productive discussion— the rules that will make that discussion productive. Also beware of total silence—unless you see rapt attention, as happens when you read aloud to the class. In a room where children have learned that the teacher wants silence, the teacher will get it, but then the question is: How many of these silent souls have learned to drift away into their own thoughts and be silent but absent? So the issue becomes not disrespect of you but how to get a group to function productively—kids participating, but in a respectful, thoughtful, and productive way.

Dottie

☜

CHAPTER 2

The Teacher's Role in a Learner-Centered Classroom

This semester I feel like I am supposed to give up "control" and let students make decisions and choices. Yet when I don't reinforce certain limitations, I'm criticized . . .

Rebecca

The child said, "I don't want to do that." What do I do? I am getting stuck with the idea that this is a learner-centered classroom and what the role of the teacher actually is . . .

Lisa

∽   Learner-centered classroom defined

∽   Authoritarian approach

∽   Learning from an eggshell

∽   The math of model houses

∽   Facilitating choice

∽   Making learning deep

∽   Learning centers

∽   Teachers as valid diagnosticians

∽   Give time to explore

∽   Let materials teach

∽   Watch and listen

∽   Dramatic play for youngers and olders

∞   A disruptive child

∞   Literature groups

∞   Spelling and punctuation

Dear Lisa,

Thanks for the detailed journal. Beginnings are so hard!

You are concerned right now about what to do as a teacher when children say to you, "I don't want to do that." Since it's a learner-centered classroom, what is your response? An excellent question, without an easy answer!

A learner-centered classroom doesn't mean that kids get to do anything they want. It only means that the work stems as much as possible from the children's interests, that it is thought out in terms of what these children, as a group and as different individuals, can do, what their individual and different approaches to learning are, what areas of the huge range of possible subject matter grip them, stir their individual passions, turn on their individual energies—and that provision is made for all these differences. A tall order, but child-centeredness means that we recognize and value the individual differences of children and that a one-size-fits-all lesson or a one-size fits-all mandated curriculum won't work well. Corollaries of a child-centered approach include that we work toward children's developing their own self-discipline as opposed to the teacher-directed approach.

When you think about it, an authoritarian approach is really about dependency. It says to the child, "Do what I tell you. Obey my rules. I take responsibility for your learning." It sends a message that the child is not capable of taking care of herself, of being responsible for her own learning. That's not what we want. We want children to be lifelong learners. We want them to know that they can learn even when we are not there. The power is theirs. So we start right from the beginning, working toward helping the child become self-disciplined and self-responsible.

But you are still the teacher. You have the final say on what may or may not be done. The children need you as authority figure (boundary setter) when they can't handle it themselves. In fact, it is helpful to them that you exercise this final control because, after all, they are still children and your presence and authority make things safe for them.

Does it sound contradictory? It is hard sometimes to figure out when to say, "Do it your way" and when to say, "No. Do it this way." How do you decide? In general, I tried to use the rule "Will something be learned from this activity"? If the answer was "Possibly," I'd say, "Yes." If the answer was "No," it couldn't be done. For instance, kids would sometimes bring in a game and want to play it during project time. I'd ask them what they thought they'd learn from playing it. If they could identify something, I'd say okay. If not, I'd say, "Save it for recess."

Of course, it's always tricky. Because who knows what might be learned from a given experience? We can't always predict! But if you've looked hard at your kids—as a group and as individuals, and if you've planned a classroom that offers a variety of possibilities for interesting learning as well as provided for a variety of entries into learning, and if you really allow choice, chances are you'll not have lost many opportunities for learning.

I agree with your assessment of what projects should be. They don't necessarily have to connect to something else, but if learning is to be deep, projects should be seriously thought out and normally, by age seven or eight, should take more than a day or two to complete. A bit here and a bit there is not likely to provide much learning.

The eggshell experiment could be an interesting one. What will they get out of it? you ask. You ask the right teacher question. I suggest, the satisfaction of setting up an experiment themselves and of seeing the results of their own work. It might go in a number of directions depending on what they see and what extending questions occur to them or occur to you that they might also be curious about. What I wondered about right away when I read your description was: Would vinegar wear away anything else beside an eggshell? What would it do to a piece of fabric? Color of the fabric? A piece of metal? I know vinegar mixed with (I think) baking soda will polish either silver or brass—it's in my cookbook! Maybe it would be good to introduce the cookbook as a reference source (research!), or maybe it would be more fun just to try it out. Something to be learned whichever route you take.

And that last "wonder" of mine led me to another wonder. I wonder what it is about vinegar that makes it do what it does. Then think about vinegar as salad dressing—the kinds of vinegar there are, where they come from, how they're made. Could we make some in the classroom? Vinegar, incidentally, will not mix with oil, and that might lead you to the properties of oil. It would be fascinating; depends on your excitement about it and how the kids pick up on it. That's the role of teacher—starting with the kids' interest and then helping to maintain it and to expand the inquiry.

Would you agree that the eggshell could lead to quite a few days of real work, real deep learning? It turns out to be the starting rather than the ending of the work.

Note, too, that I didn't come up with answers. In fact, I don't have them all. That's part of the fun of it—and part, the most important part perhaps, of the learning. Here are our questions; how can we go about finding out the answers? The essence of thinking, the essence of science, the essence of research. Isn't that what we want? And all from an eggshell and a little vinegar and no textbook!

The model of the house two children were building? What did they need to know—or to find out in order to make the model? Did they make a plan? Is there a scale? What measurement is going on? Will they put in electric lights or bells? Furniture? How many people will live in this house? How big are the model people? Are the rooms big enough to accommodate them? Can they get through the doors with an armload of groceries? Can they see out the windows? If it's a two-story house, how do they get from the first to the second floor? How wide, how high do stairs need to be?

You can see all the possibilities for both the development of ideas and the meaningful practice of skills. Kids making a model house might need to measure their own rooms at home, compare their measurements, think about the placement of kitchen to dining room, measure, measure—lengths, widths, height of ceilings.

A suggestion on scale. At about eight or nine years, kids can understand and use a scale of 1 inch on the model representing 1 foot in real life. Anything more complicated probably needs saving for later. I suggest you start kids by having them cut out of file-folder-weight paper the people who will live in the house. Then these bodies can be used to measure the workable dimensions for the structure.

So this could be a superb project, with all sorts of possibilities. Again, the teacher role is to help all this happen. To see the possibilities for learning— to ask the questions, make the comments that stimulate the child's thinking—and to provide the cardboard, tape, and glue!

I'm glad you now have books for the literature groups. I'm surprised there were not enough copies. Usually four or five copies of a title are enough. These can often be borrowed from other teachers or from branch public libraries. The public library might be a good source. (Be sure to keep a list of books you borrow; inside each book you lend a kid, write "copy 1," "copy 2," etc., and keep that list.)

You express concern about whether the spider study will hold the children's interest. I would think it would—especially if the kids can collect the spiders themselves. If you find there's no interest, don't do it. Find something else.

Dottie

∞

Dear Lisa,

Thanks again for such a useful journal. You keep thinking, questioning, and critiquing. Good for you.

Another "What to do about" question. A kid starts a project, gets bored with it, and starts something else—or doesn't start something else.

Beware of "boring." It usually indicates one of two things: (l) The child finds a project too hard and needs support for continuing. "Let's take a look at your project. How far have you gotten? What are you trying to find out? Maybe you need a different book? A different material? What if we changed the way you've planned this? Would that work? Do you need a partner to help you?" Or else (2) The child's vision hasn't enlarged. "We made a lot of paper. Now what?"

Possible intervention for paper making. You to the kids, "Tell me some of what you learned. I see. What happened when you added more of . . . [reflecting in more detail on the experience]. What if you added some rags or straw, or string, grass, twigs? Could we use your paper for paper sculpture? [extensions for further experimentation] What kind of paper is a wasp's "paper" nest? What's rice paper? Why is some paper slick, some fuzzy? How could we find out?" [Research. The connecting of print research to the experience.] And, of course, check the museums, art galleries. There may be exhibits of professional paper work. Do you see how you can begin with the hands-on activity and then perhaps expand it?

And, of course, if none of this takes, then the question is to help the child see what he's learned, perhaps document it in some way (a report, oral or written; a "how to make paper" book), bring it to closure, and help the child choose his next study project.

To sum up: in both cases of "It's boring," the role for the teacher is to enable the child to progress—extend, deepen inquiry, or sum up and move on to a new inquiry.

The situation needs to be viewed not as a failure of the child but as the need for a teacher intervention.

You can expect to get some "It's boring" some of the time from some of the kids, but you will minimize it if you remember that choice requires facilitating. It doesn't happen just by itself.

There are three ways a teacher facilitates choice. (1) Begin by helping the student think about what she is really interested in learning about so that she makes a good choice. (2) Having made her choices, she may then need help with the process of carrying it out. Carrying out a choice includes thinking through what materials will be needed, what people might be interviewed or consulted, and what books might be wanted, then making a plan of action. The plan may include the order of doing and, in a group, how the work will be shared, keeping track of progress and the method of reporting results. (3) During the work, check in with the kid to see that the project moves along, and ask those questions and make those comments that may lead to deeper thinking as well as to paths for study not originally thought of—the new questions that are frequently the most exciting.

I remember once a child painting a beautiful red bird copied from a book of Audubon prints. His original interest was in the act of painting. When the bird was done, he showed it to the class. Several children got really excited, and a small group formed to paint more birds. In the process of painting and modeling in clay, they found new questions—How do birds fly? How do they swim? How do they chew their food if they have no teeth? Were dinosaurs their ancestors? Why did Audubon kill them before he painted them? None of these questions were part of the first child's thought. His work, shared with the class, led to new investigations and new learnings.

When we're talking of planning, we're talking of older kids—maybe eight- or nine-year-olds and up. With little kids it's different. They don't have enough experience to make a long-range plan. For them, the work and the questions to think about flow from the possibilities inherent in the materials you put out (the sand and the water, the blocks). Remember also that a plan may change or evolve as kids work and learn more about their subject. But the general principle holds. Help the child make a good choice, facilitate her carrying it out through helping make a plan ("I will work with Freddie; I will work alone"), gathering resources ("I will need more big blocks"), asking the questions as she works that deepen and make the work even more compelling.

Incidentally, I found that kids often chose to do what their friends were doing—which is okay as long as the project really interests both of them and as long as they understand that you expect real investment and hard work.

You ask about learning centers as a way to organize a classroom. They may work fine. The ones I've seen—and of course I haven't seen them all—have frequently had very shallow activities, usually set up by the teacher; often with written instructions of what to do. They have seemed to me to be a nod toward child-centeredness without actually being it, their activities framed as play rather than as work, time out from the assumed unpleasant but necessary "real school" learning of reading and writing, or simply used to provide games that teach the narrow skills of arithmetic or print decoding.

You could, of course, think them out better, design them to last over several days and make them more open ended—that is, put out materials that children can use in a variety of ways so they explore their own ideas and discover information (art materials—painting, collage and construction, print making; pattern blocks without instruction cards, Lego™).

The objectives, however you organize your room, should be (1) to work from kids' interests, (2) to have a discovery focus for the work, (3) to support sustained work, and (4) to nurture deep learning. I also liked having kids do a final project or summation of what they learned. It gave a sense of accomplishment and provided closure.

And you are right, in a classroom there should always be something to do—painting, clay, weaving, wood construction, reading, writing.

Yes, our kids really are friendly. Glad you like that! Their friendliness comes from their self-confidence and the assumption, based on their CPE experience, that adults will consider them worth talking with and will be respectful of their ideas.

Dottie

∞

Dear Ellen,

It was wonderful to see you today in the classroom. You are so perceptive. You see the choices, you weigh them, you jump in, you experiment!

A few comments:

Gauging the different levels, without tests. Do it by observation and notetaking. You are already noticing! Trust your teacher judgment. Your observations will be as accurate—more so—and more timely for designing your teacher planning than any paper and pencil test will be. Here are some observations to make.

The complex drawing versus the simple. The one-sentence versus the three-sentence story the child tells you about his drawing. The writing/not writing of the name. You read to the kids. Who predicts what will happen next? (Has a sense of story line?) Familiarity with conventions ("reads" from the front to the back of the book). "Reads" the pictures and makes up a story to go with them. Notices that the story is in the print and reads some of it. You might want to have a look at *Assessing Literacy with the Learning Record*.[5] It will give you some of the benchmarks appropriate in a developmental fashion for young children.

It was good that you noticed that your "leading question" about the guinea pig was not useful. A more open-ended question—one allowing for a wider range of observation—would be: "What do you notice about the guinea pig?" and then say, "Uh, huh. What else do you notice?" Or, "That's interesting. Tell me more about it."

A good way to circulate around the room is to start such a group with the "noticing" and then say, "I'm going to check out the block area. I'll be back soon. You could start drawing the guinea pig, if you like, and when I come back you can tell me more things you noticed." And then you go on to the next group, knowing this first one is settled in and has a way to proceed.

Dottie

☙

Dear Ellen,

Lesson plans. It's too soon for you to write them. You need to watch the kids and listen to them as they work with the materials so you get some idea of the possibilities. You are going to design plans that provide for exploration and for inquiry learning, so right now you need to discover the nature of a child's inquiry process.

You are watching the kids at the magnet table. What kind of magnets did the teacher put out? Were they all the same? If not, what kind of exploration do you think she thought might happen if she set up the environment a certain way? What did the children actually do with the magnets? What questions (usually not spoken out loud) do you think they were investigating? What materials might you add another day to help in their exploration?

Don't intervene too fast. When kids are working with new materials, they need time to explore freely—more than once. They will be learning a lot by experimenting without instruction from you (other than not to drop the magnets, because they break inside and won't work). And again, as the teacher, your task is to watch, listen, and maybe say, "What are you noticing? Ah! Tell me more." Try not to push for quick results that you can see but build your interventions around what their questions and misconceptions seem to be.

I remember in my first year of teaching I put out rods for kids to "play" with and was in a panic because my classroom management skills were so poor I could never get over to their table to see what they were doing and "teach" rods. Finally, after three or four weeks, I brought a box of rods to a whole class meeting, hid all but one rod behind my back and said, "Who can tell me something about rods?" The response was immediate and whole class. They knew the colors, the smallest, the largest, the ones that were the same size, they could seriate them—in short, all the things I would have "taught" didn't need teaching. The materials and the freedom to explore and build did the teaching.

Not that I'm recommending you stay away for weeks, but just know that the materials will teach—so long as kids are free to explore with them.

Dottie

∞

Dear Ellen,

More on "lesson" plans. I had another idea about the cooking today.

You noticed correctly that for these four-year-olds the urge to pour and mix was very strong. In fact, it seemed to be the major point of connection for them—the process more than the idea of a finished product to eat. Your plan could now include adding some muffin tins and bowls to both the sand table and the water table. It will help meet the need to pour and mix, and it will give a useful experience in seeing what happens when pour and mix are done with different materials. Science, again! The possibilities are endless!

Lia is a very advanced writer, as you point out. Perhaps her restlessness and interruptions at other activities may be her way of telling you that right now her focus is on writing, and that's where she's ready to grow. I would encourage her writing a lot and go light on other activities. It will all come after awhile.

My youngest, who taught himself to read when he was three, suffered through the first weeks of traditional first grade. They wouldn't give him a book because they hadn't yet tested him to see what level he was on! I put him in a learner-centered school. He did nothing but read and write for a long time. There was a hunger that needed to be satisfied before he could release energy for math and socializing. He wrote millions of little books, some in languages he invented (his older sister was studying French at the time), and he carried them with him in a big paper bag everywhere he went. The rest of the curriculum came later. Why not? We think we have to be so lockstep and sequential in school. Why? Why not take our cues from the children? Where are their interests? Their passions? As long as all the possibilities are there in the classroom and they can explore, they'll come to it when they're ready.

Re: Steven. You did fine. Another time you might take him by the hand and say very quietly, "You seem all excited today. Can you tell me about it?" In the telling he might be able to get rid of some of his anger. Has he a friend in the class he might take to a corner and tell him about it? It might help. Worth a try.

Dottie

∞

Dear Ellen,

So glad you got a chance to observe kids working in the block area. Yes, indeed, there were different "levels"—some kids working alone, others with one or more friends. An excellent opportunity for kids to learn to negotiate the process of working together—an important skill schools can help teach, yes?

Also good that you saw the process of "kids teaching kids" as they helped each other build. Good, too, that you recognized some of the science—experience with weight and balance—and the math. That in building the kids were experiencing, over time, the meaning of same size, longer/shorter, twice as long as, half as long as—the attributes of shapes—and deepening the understanding of what those attributes mean (e.g., that both cylinders and rectangular boxes will hold up bridges and roofs, that if cylinders are used for a floor the floor

Figure 2.1 Block building in the kindergarten. The boy solves the problem of balance and strength by massing lots of blocks.

will roll, whereas rectangular boxes make a stable floor). Cylinders set up as an inclined plane make a bumpy ride for a car, but a wedge makes an excellent slide. Shapes are related to functions in the real world of architecture and the design of everyday objects. Learning is a lot richer this way than it would be in a whole-class lesson of naming and describing shapes.

The blocks are teaching, aren't they? You, the teacher, have little to do—other than to provide the materials and the space and support the work (with your comments, questions, and provisioning.)

*Figure 2.2 The girl has discovered that balance is all that's
required for height and has created a more economic structure.*

Glad your brownies turned out. A good learning experience to see how
the batter looked different uncooked, cooked, and burned! Might you call
this a science lesson?

Dottie

P.S. Use our "possible learnings" form to analyze the cooking experience.
What academic learnings—detail the science, the math, the language—what
social learnings, personal connections, and growth? Share at lunch. I'll ask
Lisa to copresent for the upper grades.

∞

Dear Ellen,

You ask, "Up till what age should one have a dramatic play area in the room?"

I really don't know. Certainly through first and possibly through second grade. You have already commented on the learnings that happen in such an area—the trying on of adult characteristics and relationships—fathers and mothers, children and parents, babies, pets. You can even hear the tones of voice change! As children try on these roles, they learn more about their world; it helps them move from ego-centeredness to other-centeredness. We really can't be other-centered until we can put ourselves into another's place—as the kids are doing!

Last week the teacher added a suitcase and a fireman's hat. You noticed how that expanded the "play."

As kids get older, this kind of play seems "babyish" to them. They're ready to write/act/read plays and take more planned-out-in-advance roles; that's an extension of the earlier experience.

P.S. Did you notice the doll-babies are of both genders and several races? P.P.S. Would you present at lunch what you've discovered about possible learnings in the dramatic play area? And take a look at the painting area. What might possibly be learned in painting? Use the three-category work-sheet (Appendix D) to detail possible academic learnings, possible social learnings, possible "personal connection" learnings. Lisa has agreed to do the same for painting with older kids. Can you think, as you watch the little ones, what some of the learnings and extensions of learnings might be for the older kids, and how those learnings might grow more naturally, easily from early painting experiences? But perhaps this belongs after you and Lisa present and we discuss.

Dottie

∽

Dear Lisa,

You asked, "Should I interrupt an already-underway curriculum unit on Africa to take up the kids' questions about the construction they saw on yesterday's walk?" An excellent question.

I think you're wondering about losing momentum and immersion in a unit already underway versus taking advantage of a question that a child has because of the experience of the walk. Good thinking. These are the issues!

Figure 2.3 A five-year-old sets the table for dinner in the dramatic play area.

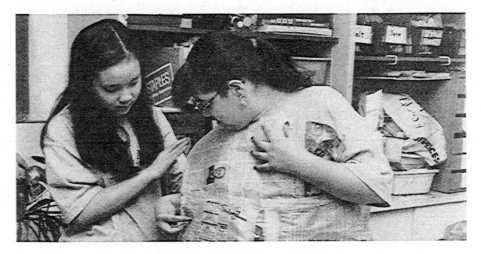

Figure 2.4 Fifth/sixth grader Kristine checks a paper pattern on Iris for a costume they will now cut from cloth. They explained, "This is part of our search project. A search project is something that interests you or something you don't know a lot about. We looked in books and on the computer. We saw that in ancient Greek times the gods played a big part, and the people always got in trouble. We wrote a play. We changed the gods a little. We made it a comedy. We rounded up a cast of twelve. Then we did the read-throughs. We made drawings of the costumes, then measured the kids. Danielle did the math and translated it into yardage. The stage manager decided the props. We're measuring the auditorium. We'll paint on cardboard and flip them over; the paint crew will make eight scenes on four cardboards. Iris and I are the directors."

You have options. You might want to take time out for an exploratory discussion. "Yesterday, on our walk, Mark noticed the big crane by our street. Did other people notice it? Were you curious about what was going to be built?" Gives you a chance to evaluate whether the question held to the next day or was only of passing interest.

If there is some interest, you could ask, "How might we find out?" Perhaps a small committee might be formed. This research might be a few days' project for a small group, or if the interest seems wider/deeper, you might (1) have two curricula going simultaneously (kids would need to choose and regroup), or (2) if you are near the end of the first curriculum, you and the kids might decide to put the new curriculum on hold for just a few weeks. Some kids might opt to do both, setting Monday and Tuesday aside for the construction and Wednesday and Thursday for Africa. All kinds of possibilities, a matter of organization for you.

Re: the African structure and a strategy for building it. Not an issue for frustration. View it as an opportunity for learning. If there are good builders in the room, they might come to help. Or you could flick off the light, explain the difficulty you and the child are having, and get a small group to come and try out different techniques. Look on it less as a "teacher must provide answers" situation and more as a "how can I help create a discovery, exploratory child-help-child situation." Enjoy the exploration yourself. It is far more important for learning that a number of children explore and try out various ways to solve the problem than that the structure gets built. The problem solving engages the brain, results in risk taking, thinking, hypotheses formation, rejection of some hypotheses, and formulating new ones based on the failures of previous efforts. Much more will be learned than if the teacher supplies the answer.

Dottie

P.S. Teachers talking at children is not teaching.

∞

Dear Lisa,

You seem to feel quite strongly that Meg should have handled the disruptive child right then and there in her own classroom rather than sending him to her buddy teacher to cool off. It seems to me that having a buddy teacher is an excellent idea and that Meg used her buddy appropriately.

How would you handle a disruptive child? Take away recess? Argue with him? Tell him "no" sixty times? Call his parents? Once is enough to tell a child "no." Recognizing that he can't handle the classroom at that moment and sending him with work to another room recognizes the situation and avoids the authority clash that you need to avoid, especially with preadolescents! Most kids want to be in their own room, and when they see a few times what loss of their self-control results in, they'll exercise self-control more readily. Later, when you don't have the whole class, you may also want to conference with the child and help him devise a plan to control his own behavior.

If the behavior continues, you may want a parent-teacher-child conference to make an agreed-on (three-way agreement!) plan and a second conference a few weeks later to check on progress and the appropriateness of the plan. Notice that this kind of conference is not designed to give the parents a chance to berate their child in front of the teacher or the teacher to berate the child in front of the parents. It's a serious problem-solving session with all three concerned parties putting their heads together for a workable plan that should be written down and signed by everyone. The follow-up is also important, especially (or at least equally) important if all has gone well. You'll want a chance to congratulate the child for his success (or progress) in front of the same audience that his misbehavior was discussed. If all is well, and the child agrees, you could do the second conference over the phone.

The child who wrote about not having friends. Was it a good piece of writing? Might you talk with her about it as a piece of writing? How powerful writing is when it comes from our own personal experience and feelings! At the same time, you might want to watch her social interactions. Is there something she does that invites loneliness? Is there an intervention needed? First, observe the child and gather some data.

Re: picking on the special-education kids by your fifth/sixth graders. Not permitted—and should be dealt with as a whole-class discussion immediately if it happens again. You could still deal with it now, even though a number of days have passed, by saying, "You know what? I've been thinking about what happened last week and it really bothered me, so let's talk about it." You might also want to do a deeper discussion about feelings and attitudes—writing both anti- and sympathetic viewpoints on chart paper without comment, accepting everything that's said, including all the misinformation that people have about Special Ed kids. Then the class can discuss each item brought up—and the evidence, if any, that supports their viewpoint. Maybe some research is indicated. They may want to have the Special Ed teacher, or someone from an agency, come to discuss the issues. Some children will have had personal experience. You'll judge by the discussion how far you want to carry it. Here's a chance, once again, to deal not only with a situation, but to use the event as a learning opportunity. Do a lesson plan for it now. Think ahead. Consider the possibilities, and you'll be ready to deal with it.

Dottie

∞

Dear Lisa,

Good stuff to talk about in your journal. It sounds as if your literature group is working out wonderfully well! Exciting that they want to keep reading! That's one of the things we're after!

You ask how to get kids involved. You did! The "Oooo, do I have to?" is typical of this age. It used to fry me when I heard it. How dare they not be enthusiastic about what I'm enthusiastic about! But then I realized what it was about, and in general you can smile sweetly and say, "Yes, you do have to!" At the same time, you want to spark enthusiasm. Step 1 is to have read the books yourself! Don't leave the development of discussion and questions to chance. Know yourself where exciting parts are in the book, where interesting ideas come up, or questions are raised.

After that, as a starter, if each group is to read two chapters for homework, you might want to look again at the two chapters in each book and give them one question to think about as they read. "There's something special to look for in this chapter, a kind of clue for what will happen next. See if you can find it." Of course, you mostly want them to raise their own questions, but learning how to raise important questions requires some modeling, so some of your ideas and some of theirs are both appropriate.

You might also want to consider circulating among the groups to listen to the discussions, to lend sympathetic support, praising them for their great ideas, seeing if a comment or question from you would deepen their thinking— rather than to spend the whole time with one group. Circulating also gives you instant information about what group work skills they need help with so that you know how to design your minilessons or other interventions.

As you circulate and listen in, the kids will pick up on your enthusiasm and feel good about what they're doing because you feel good about it. You show them you think their reading work is important since you come around to pay attention to it!

Re: writing. You ask about spelling, content, etc. What's the structure of the writing program? Do they use writing workshop technique—writing, sharing with the class, critiquing as Ellen described for Win's room?

Because you are right. Content should come first. I used a writing workshop method. I made a list each time of the kids who shared their writing and what suggestions the class made. Then the next day I conferenced first with those children to remind them of the suggestions made. I asked which they planned to use and if they'd decided where to put the additions, what was to be deleted, and so on. I began to do it this way when I saw that numbers of kids read their stories to the class and then never went back to their first draft. I didn't want to require that they make changes, but I did want them to feel that reading their writing and considering their audience's ideas was a serious piece of the work.

When someone said their story was done, then I'd help with mechanics. Have them start by circling the words they want spelling help with. You'll be amazed, as I was, that they could catch almost all their errors! Visual memory is quite good by the third/fourth grade. After that, I sat with them and we'd look at each word and discuss how smart their invented spelling was and how crazy Standard English spelling is. Then I'd give the *standard* spelling (I tried to avoid "correct.")

Eight- and nine-year-olds usually can handle periods, capital letters, and question marks without help. If you find several need help with quotation marks or paragraphing, do a minicourse for that group and meet maybe three days in a row. Let them bring books, or paragraphs, to find out how quotation marks are used. Let them try to fix their own writing. Then have them exchange a page with one other person in the group to see if they agree on the change. They can explain to each other why they did what they did and you only need to be the final arbiter. (I gave a little graduation certificate to eight- and nine-year-olds after each course.)

At some point, teach dictionary skills. Let the child make several guesses about how a word might be spelled and then look for it.

What about the child who writes well and spells badly? If she also reads well, and my guess is she does, she probably has the standard spelling in her head and simply isn't focused on it. It may be time to help her focus and discover what she knows. Try it. No harm in seeing.

I suggest you point out to her the possibility that she has the standard spelling in her head and tell her you'd like to work intensively with her for a while. Ask her to start each writing period by taking an old piece of writing and circling the words she thinks are not standard on a half-page.

Then sit with her and see what happens. Can she improve her sound/symbol sense? Can she think of words that rhyme with this one and how the rhymes are spelled? Are there tricky words like *there* and *their* that she gets mixed up, and are there tricky ways to remember them? (A child once told me his way of remembering was that *here* was the opposite of *there* and so belonged to it and was inside it.)

Where you see the whole class has a particular problem with those tricky words, you can even do a ten-minute discussion of those words and the strategies kids use to spell them.

Thanks for a very good journal. I love to dialogue on my favorite subject. Thanks for giving me the opportunity!

Dottie

⊙

CHAPTER 3

Ranging Far and Wide: Questions About Everything

෯

Josh to Kevin, age five: Was the pumpkin that big when your Daddy bought it for you last week?

Kevin: Oh, no! It was MUCH smaller!

Amy, age six, at apple picking time: I'm putting these into my bag so they'll get big and fat.

James, age six: Soon it will smell like snow.

- ෯ Pumpkins and apples
- ෯ Touchable science
- ෯ Blocks and the subway
- ෯ The park as laboratory
- ෯ Looking for strengths
- ෯ A dinosaur unit
- ෯ Adjusting the classroom
- ෯ Getting perspective on yourself
- ෯ Seeing your growth, allowing yourself some failures
- ෯ Reading, writing, discussions should start with kids' ideas
- ෯ Teaching the care of materials
- ෯ Art as an entry to learning

∞   Establishing the classroom culture—modeling, role playing, conflict resolution

∞   More on discipline

Dear Nicky,

Apple picking is so good! Can you make a list of possible learnings for math and science as well as for writing/reading? Don't forget fractions that happen when kids share an apple. What happens that kids can see while cooking applesauce? Watch and listen to what they do/say as they cook. What questions or comments might you as teacher ask to help them observe more closely? Also weigh a few apples and then allow them to dry. What do you think will happen to their weight? Would you ask the kids to hazard some guesses before the apples dry—or rot? Why do you suppose some might dry while others rot?

Autumn is also a good time to buy a pumpkin and look at pumpkin insides and make pumpkin cupcakes and watch a pumpkin rot. This last activity will be incredibly interesting!

Integrated curriculums help make sense of the "subjects." You can relate science, social studies, math, and language skills together.

Dottie

∞

Dear Johnisha,

Re: science—think about what's age appropriate: You could study constellations. But will it be a one-shot deal, or will it lead to deeper understanding? I wonder. Especially when our kids can't even see the stars at night! I wouldn't say no, but I wonder.

In general, start science from the child's touchable, viewable, immediate environment. Go to the park, even if they've been there many times before. Learning takes place with repeated experience. Collect stuff. Look at stuff. Be the wind and blow a seed. Bring back a feather. How does the water look when a duck is swimming? What happens when you throw in a stone?

And then discuss what you saw when you get back to school. Let the science develop from searching for the answers to their questions about the experience. Appropriate hands-on activities in the room may also raise new questions. That's what we hope for! Bring in books *after* the initial experiencing. The books will be more relevant and more understandable because of the experience. And if you bring them in after rather than before, the kids' questions will be wider. *Books do expand information, but sometimes*

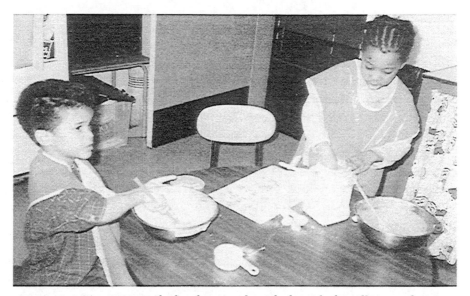

Figure 3.1 Two K/1s cook the class snack with the aid of an illustrated recipe, leveled ingredient containers, and occasional assist from the teacher. Older children can explore in depth the chemistry of cooking. Children grow in awareness of the changes that happen as they pour, blend, and bake. Opportunities for science, math, and language are many.

they also narrow the inquiry because the author is often providing information that, if it comes too soon, stifles questions and hypothesizing.

The math that you'll do (sorting, counting, measuring) also takes on meaning as these processes are used with real things.

Your cooking should also be science—and math and language! Let's talk about that at lunch. What science, what math, what language can you see in cooking?

Do informal science when they arrive in the morning. "It's colder today. Autumn is like that, and when winter comes. . . ." (Imagine—in my old school we used to have kids memorize the seasons apart from experiencing them!) Take advantage of windy days and rainy days and clouds to call kids' attention to the changes. All of this is natural, ongoing, sensible science—not artificial one-shot deals, not paper and pencil work that kids do without real understanding of what it's about. I hope you've got animals. Someone may bring in a shell or a special rock. Use that.

Dottie

Dear Ellen,

Sounds as if the block work is going very well! Thanks for presenting at
lunch today. Your intervention with Willie when his train wouldn't fit into
the tunnel he'd made was just right. "How might you change that so it will
work?"—instead of providing the solution, "Try making it bigger." Excellent open-ended question—designed to make the widest possible space for
his thinking.

And how great that the teacher had you take a small group to visit a subway entrance to see how the trains come in, how they "fit" into the space,
using the block work to look at the real world more closely, then reproducing that world again in blocks to understand it even better.

And now that the children are building a variety of houses and towers,
you'll take them for neighborhood walks—to see in more detail the real
world that they're reproducing in blocks. They'll look more closely, won't
they, since looking relates to *their* work.

You'll notice during the semester how trips to the zoo, the park, the air-
port will result in new block building—and will deepen the children's
understanding of the world.

Another interesting thing to look for is how individual children connect
differently to the same experience. I remember seeing this happen one semester. Each of the five children who went on a buildings walk related to what
they saw in a different way. When they came back, one child built the foun-
tain with the fish in it, another made a curved entry to her building. The same
visit to see the same thing, yet each made his own connection to it!

Dottie

⊗

Dear Johnisha,

Your rain lesson plan (listening) is okay. Nothing wrong with it; you need
to do it for your college class. In real life, you probably wouldn't do it. It's
artificial, unrelated. Use real rain if you want them to hear it. Imitate after.
If your goal is to practice listening, do that every day in the ongoing life of
your classroom, at times when kids really need to listen and the techniques
of how to listen can be discussed and practiced in context. "I like the way
John listens. His hands are still. His feet are still. His mouth is quiet, and
he's looking at Sammy when Sammy is talking." Or "I like the way
Monique listens. I can see by her quiet face that she's found a quiet place

inside herself." Or "We need to practice listening. Fix your feet. They should be in front of you [or wherever you want them]. Fix your hands. They should be in your own lap. Close your mouth. Find the quiet place inside you" [the latter said with your own getting-quieter-and-quieter voice]. Nothing like a teacher who shouts, "Get quiet." Wouldn't you agree?

You can also practice listening in other ways. "Close your eyes. Listen hard. What sounds are you hearing?" Then, after a minute or two, "Open your eyes. Raise your hand. What did you hear?" It is truly a wonder how many sounds we miss with our own noise!

Dottie

∞

Dear Ellen,

You describe the wonderful day at the park and say you think the kids could go there every day. Yes, indeed, they could go every day. The park is a wonderful resource—a live laboratory. I used to do a Central Park curriculum with my third/fourth graders, which included science, a little history, animals, geology, plant life, architecture, maps, art, water.

This time of year use the park to study autumn. What does it look like, feel like, smell like? Look at leaves. Seeds are everywhere. They are different sizes and shapes. They're on trees and bushes and grass. They're getting ready to travel. Be the wind. Blow a dandelion head! How are other seeds traveling? Don't forget to put some burrs in the collection that the kids can bring back to discuss. How might a burr travel? And remember, don't *tell* the kids. Ask them to look and say what they see. Ask them what they notice. And praise them for "good eyes." They'll look even harder!

Use your Central Park seeds for math—count, sort (math sets). Compare these seeds with seeds from pumpkin, corn. Look at the insides of green peppers, apples, tomatoes, kiwis. Where are the seeds? Draw the patterns. Looking at seeds inside fruit led one second grader to ask, "How did the seeds get in there?" Another, hearing that question, asked, "How will they get out?"

You, of course, don't answer those questions, even if you know. You say: "Hey, good questions! How might we find out?"

Could we grow outdoor seeds inside? Would they all grow? If the kids are curious, have them plant some.

Look at the leaves—sort by size, shape. Can the kids think of their own categories for sorting? Look at the edges. Measure lengths and areas. Make graphs of smallest to biggest. Incidentally, what do we mean by "biggest"? Is a leaf that is longer but thinner bigger than one that is shorter but fatter? Again, you don't decide, but it might make a learning thinking-packed discussion!

Do rubbings to see textures and make more explicit the structure of leaves—spines and veins.

Look at barks. Compare similarities and differences. What does bark do for the tree? What about roots?

Why are squirrels burying acorns? Do they remember where they've buried them? What other animals can you find in the park and where? Don't forget to look under rocks and do a little digging.

Central Park is part of the flyway south, so go to the reservoir and check out the birds. Extend the study of birds (including their bones, which are interesting).

You should run with the kids down hills and go over the bridges and look at the water. Does running downhill feel different from running on a flat place? In what way? Why might that be? What differences do you notice when you look at water from different perspectives? (Science made vivid, made real, made relevant because it stems from experience.) Allow time for play after work so the emotional pull of the park can be deeper. Discuss their feelings. What do the kids like about the park? Would it be as much fun if it were flat?

You should go back in the winter, particularly on a snowy day. What differences are there? What can you learn about snow?

Go again in the spring and note the differences.

When the weather is nice, you can take the writing notebooks out and write in the park. Take books and read to the kids and have them read in the park. You can also take paint and paper. Attach the sheets with masking tape at one end to a heavy cardboard backing. Art is a "subject" in its own right. It also contributes to science learning. What do things really look like? How do you know what's behind something, closer or farther away? How do you show that something is three dimensional? Observation skills, wouldn't you agree?

The rules for a park visit have to be explained and enforced. You can play first and work later or vice versa. I found they could really work first at age eight. "We'll write for 20 minutes. You check your work with us and then you may play."

Also plan for safety issues. The kids need to be visible at all times; set a boundary around the area you are studying and be sure they know it. Have partners who are responsible for each other, and do a head count periodically.

So you see, the park can be a curriculum. All year long. You don't have to go there every day, for the work in the park brings back work to be done in the classroom. It extends to museums, gets enlarged with books, plantings, and classroom terrariums and includes all the subject and skill areas! This would be a curriculum rich in academics, stemming from the child's environment and taught experientially where the child can see it, feel it, and use it as a starting point for further investigation.

Dottie

∞

Dear Ellen,

I'm glad you got to go to the park again and do some observations and collecting. The idea of a collage of natural materials was a good one. Perhaps, rather than "What are you making?" as a teacher intervention, you might want to try the more open-ended question, "Tell me about your collage." They may not be "making" anything. They may be enjoying the glueing or enjoying the aesthetics of the materials—colors, shapes, textures. All legitimate "learnings," wouldn't you agree? The "what are you making" question narrows their vision and you may miss altogether what their thinking is. Stick with those nifty questions—"Tell me about it. Tell me more." Good for a starter in almost any activity! Their response will tell you what to do or say next.

Comparing seeds and describing: a good seed activity and good open-ended questions! The next questions after "What do you notice?" and "Tell us more" depend on what the children saw. Again, work from their ideas rather than from yours. When they come up with the wrong hypothesis—which you hope they do—you say, "That's interesting. Why do you think that?" "Does anyone have another idea?" "What makes you think that?" and if there are disagreements, "How could we find out?"—and voila! You have research (with or without "fair test"). I never liked to introduce fair test, hoping the kids would suggest multiple variables and then, after the experiment's ambiguous results, I could ask the question, which would help them see the need for a fair test.

If they hang on to their wrong hypotheses with childlike tenacity, you may want to think of additional experiences you could provide to help "correct" these. Saying, "Wrong, here's the right answer," won't convince them anyhow. (See Lillian Weber's article for an example of how this was done with a guinea pig.)[6]

You are getting up your courage and taking risks nicely. Good for you.

Dottie

P.S. A good definition of an open-ended question is a question that invites a number of different responses as opposed to a question that has only one answer.

∞

Dear Johnisha,

It is exciting to see things happening in the classroom that your texts said would happen. The natural conversations with children like these you had on the city bus are the best! And what they show is that when children are engaged in the real world, having real experiences, the conversations become real, too.

That's what we want to duplicate in the classroom.

The child I watched at the sand table is wonderful! A whole work time productively engaged is marvelous for her and should be acknowledged. A teacher needs to try to figure out why she was so engaged with this material and try to maximize those activities in which she engages. Minimize the hard ones at this point. She needs to feel good about herself, successful. The teachers need to feel good about her, too. Then you can help her work a little at a time on the hard stuff. She'll be better able to do it with some success already hers.

Dottie

∞

Dear Johnisha,

Re: meeting all the needs of different students, especially pre-K, who seem (at first) to need so much . . . like the one who wanted your constant attention for writing while Joshua wanted you to read his book to him. What to do?

You have a number of options—several of which you figured out for yourself and tried! You start a kid (as you did), then tell her you're going to help others but you'll come back in about 5 minutes to see if she needs more help (reassurance). You tell Joshua, as you did, who's before him and say you'll read his book if there's time, and if there's not time, he should remind you that his book is first tomorrow (again, reassurance), and, as you did, invite him to listen to the one you are reading with Sam and Monique.

Another option is to say, "I think there won't be time for me to read with you today, but [another child] might like to read with you. Would you like to ask him?" This helps keep kids in the help-each-other-mode and nurtures their independence.

Incidentally, with eight- and nine-year-olds, the same things happen. Sometimes more kids need help from you than you can give. When I saw a line forming, I used similar options. I often put my arm around two or three kids who were waiting, and said, "Look at what Monique and I are working on. Isn't this interesting? What do you think about it?" or "Could you help us figure out what to do?" This way I was teaching several kids at once, keeping them productively busy, and still reassuring them I would get to their problem in turn.

About your feelings. One always wants to be mama, and, in part, teachers are mamas. Kids will even call you mama, expressing their feeling about who you are. But we are not only the petting, consoling, love-expressing piece of mama. We are also the supporter-toward-independence piece of mama. Kindergarten and first grade are especially hard, as you've noted. The first step into a very big world. We want them to feel safe and loved, but also to move them toward independence. So, in general, encourage, "You can do that all by yourself"—or with a friend's help.

Learning to wait is also an important learning. Done with support: "I'll check back in 5 minutes. If not today, then tomorrow."

Sharing: "Come join us. We'll all read it together."

Re: name-calling and hurting each other's feelings. You were right to stop it. You might also consider this technique. State the rule: "In our school, we don't hurt each other's feelings." Ask the complaining child if she would like to say something to the offending child and offer to come with her and to stand by. This helps children learn how to say what they feel and to deal by themselves with conflict situations. It gives the offending child a chance to learn how to respond and also to think about behavior. If you do all the reprimanding, it becomes an authority-defying situation instead of a conflict-solving one. The latter is an important learning experience.

You are right that experiencing the animals is better than just reading about them. After a period of observation and recording (usually drawing at this age and dictating to the adult the words the child may want to go with his picture), then bring the books. Now the written language will have more meaning.

Re: the difficulty of getting the kids to share at the applesauce-making table. Could they have taken turns with the process? Sharing is hard at this age. Kids are too ego-centered. Sharing can be suggested, but maybe not forced?

I remember when my daughter was at nursery school. At snack time the child whose turn it was to pass snack was told to take her own first (but to wait to eat it) and then serve the others. That way the child was assured her interest was taken care of and could be more gracious about serving the others.

Dottie

∽

Dear Johnisha,

What to do when a single child monopolizes the discussion and you see interest flagging? It's okay to cut her off: "You have so much to tell us. That's so good. Now we need to give someone else a chance."

At the other extreme, what to do when no one wants to say anything? Sometimes, after a trip, I'd say, "Tell us one thing you noticed or learned today," and I'd go right around the circle. Later we'd have the discussion.

You are right that children soon figure out what teachers want to hear and say it—especially, as you note, when right answers are valued. *How crucial to thinking and risk taking that CPE teachers value multiple possibilities, multiple solutions, or no solutions at all!*

The next step, as you know, is to think about those kids who are concerned with right answers despite our risk-encouraging atmosphere. How can we encourage them to risk?

Dottie

∽

Dear Nicky,

The encounter with Francis doesn't sound all that bad. Good you wrote it down so you could think about it more. Remember, it doesn't hurt for a kid to see that a teacher is human. If you were perfect, you would be setting up a role model for kids that they couldn't possibly hope to emulate. Not a good idea. If you feel you'd like to apologize to the kid, that's very nice. It won't diminish your authority. And remember, too, that with a kid you never lose it all out of any one incident. Keep breathing deeply!

You mention that in the name-sorting activity the girls who seemed the most "gifted" were the most active participants. Look out for "gifted"! Several of the most gifted artists I've taught were learning disabled for reading. So was an eight-year-old carpenter who could draw anything, measure anything, cut, nail, and build out of wood. It always puzzled me that a child who had such an accurate eye for visual stuff had such a hard time learning to read! Another of my eight-year-old artists/struggling readers was also a superb thinker with strong moral concerns about people and society. Definitely gifted!

Note that the name-sorting activity involved the use of print language and this involves facility with that mode of learning and the self-confidence to use it. Often a middle-class kid's strong point. You may be seeing "gifted," or at least gifted in one area. You may be seeing gender or class.

Watch for other modes through which children may show what they know and how they think. What do they show you they know through building with blocks? Through painting? Through social interactions?

Re: Anika and her distractibility: I don't know what causes it. You need to observe her in many activities and work situations to get a handle on it. You say she needs help with writing. What do you mean? No ideas to put down, or the physical act of writing? Since she's only six, she may be feeling she can't succeed in an area where adults feel she "should." If she were emotionally involved with the writing, she might be less distracted.

Does she like to draw? Would she draw a picture for you and tell you a story about it, some of which you could write down for her under the picture? If so, do that, and let her practice the handwriting piece by writing right under what you have written. There are lots more things you can do, depending on your analysis of what her strengths and interests are. Let me know.

I'm glad your cooperating teacher divides the kids into random groups (she may have nonrandomly included a few socially advanced and nonadvanced ones in each group). Avoids the smart/dumb labels and avoids cliques, also. It's okay to use different ways to organize groups, depending on how you think the particular thing will best be learned, and so long as the groups are temporary and not fixed for life. Of course, you will try to devise ways to make groups multilevel.

Figure 3.2 "If you think of him, you will start to draw him." For little ones, drawing is the story, the rehearsal before the words.

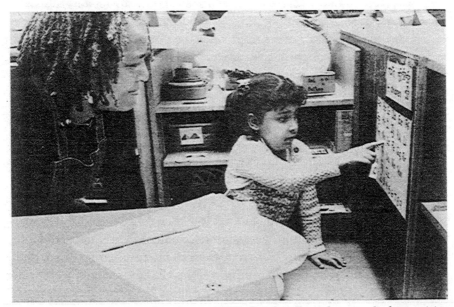

Figure 3.3 An alphabet placed at a child's height allows her to edit her writing.

Figure 3.4 With an older child, drawing has a different function. John describes his work. "I saw Scream Two. So we came to the decision. Why don't we do our own? I wrote it first in my journal. My freind helped me draw the storyboard and write the script. Cooperation was a problem. Nobody would listen. We had a meeting. We said, 'If you're not going to handle this play seriously, then you ought not be in it.' Now we have it on film."

As with the name-sorting activity, you could set the groups up by ability level for that activity, with you working with the slowest. Or you could set it up with partners, a somewhat more skilled with a somewhat less skilled partner, with you circulating to see who needs your help at that moment and how the kids are thinking about the task. The advantages of the latter method are: (1) you haven't labeled anyone, and (2) kids are learning to help each other, including learning that it's okay to receive help (many kids willingly give it, but don't receive it as willingly), and (3) you get a chance to see *how* kids work as well as *what* they can do.

Re: reading whole class, small group, individual. Each has its value and its place. We'll talk at lunch.

Dottie

⚭

Dear Ellen,

Tell me about Wally. Why do you think he is turned off to math? He "refuses to concentrate," you write. Any idea why? Is it just for math? Other areas as well? When, if ever, does he concentrate? Does it happen for particular subjects? Does the size and composition of the group he's working with have any effect? Does he do well alone, with one other person, small group, whole class? Are there things that turn him on?

Observe him for several days in various contexts and make notes. Focus particularly on any strengths for concentration you can find. We'll need to try to design interventions around his strengths. Let me know what you discover. And let's not label him a "nonconcentrator." Labeling a kid tends to keep us from looking at the details and possibly finding some good entry point. (I'm not denying his lack of concentration; just want to avoid a label.)

Dottie

⚭

Dear Ellen,

The dinosaur unit should be a good one. Kids are truly fascinated by them. Make it as "real" as you can, with lots of hands-on activities. The closest you can get to reality with dinosaurs is probably the Museum of Natural History. Have kids eyeball the models for size in terms of their own bodies. (This dinosaur is ten times taller than my partner.) It's easier to work in pairs for measurement since it's hard to see oneself.

The bones are fascinating. Does the school have a collection of large bones? It would be good to begin to collect bones and save them for your future classroom. Maybe some parent has a collection. An old-fashioned butcher, one who cuts his own meat, once gave a teacher at CPE a shoulder from a cow. What a monstrous size! Have kids bring in little bones, too. A chicken wing, leg, to look at for similarities and differences. And there are great skeleton books.

You could make a dinosaur as tall as your classroom ceiling, perhaps. From boxes. Ask the art teacher. Measure the length and height of dinosaurs on halls and walls. Kids can make small models, with papier-maché or stuffed paper. All these building projects require that kids use books, look hard at pictures, really invest themselves in the measurements, learning a lot of other dinosaur information at the same time, in ways that stick, since it's learning by doing. Flat drawing and writing is fine, too, but not sufficient to hold interest and maximize learning.

Should you or the kids cut the dinosaur shapes for the dinosaur books? That depends. As with so much teaching, there's no one right answer. It depends on what you want to accomplish. If you want beautiful cutting, you do it. If you want them to experience in another way the shape and posture of dinosaurs, then have them do it.

Why are you pairing a first and a second grader together on these books? Because you want a more experienced person to work with a less experienced one? Good idea, but competency does not necessarily correlate with chronological age. Are there not competent first graders, and second graders who need help? In a multiage classroom, you have such wonderful opportunity to give each child the experience she needs—regardless of her chronological age. Why continue the artificial boundaries of chronological age? Make use of the individual differences.

You talk about maybe having a small group do a book together. Good idea, especially at this early age, where writing is still hard for so many. How about cutting out a really large dinosaur shape for the book? Gather the group. Use a large sheet of paper. Have each kid dictate a sentence for the book. Have them read the book together. Ask them if they like what they've written. Is there anything they want to add or change? A real author's experience. Then give each child one page to draw one picture. Before you send them to draw, ask, "What might you draw to go with this sentence?" A way of getting better thought-out illustrations and another "reading" lesson on how authors and illustrators work together.

When the pages are done, you put it together. Get the group to decide on a title. And write all the authors' names on it (another lesson on books).

When they're all done, they can do a choral reading to the whole class. I think this will turn out to be a favorite book and will be read by them many times.

Dottie

∽

Dear Ellen,

I'm glad the "benching" worked. A good idea to put a finite time on it, like you did. Benched for 5 minutes. That's a manageable amount for a young child and enforceable by you. Incidentally, benching is not punishment. It is a consequence. It's directly related to recess behavior that just happened. And appropriate to the fighting. Benching gives the kid a chance to calm down and lets him know that there is an adult who will help him in an appropriate way to regain his self-control. Good judgment on your part. And yes, he will still love you. You have provided him with security by recognizing what he needed and providing it.

I think you did right to have Reginald sit with you during reading rather than allowing him to continue sitting in a nonproductive spot. Sitting with you is not punishment. In this case, it was safety—to prevent an incident you saw coming, and a quick solution, so you could go on reading with Tara.

Even sitting next to you, Reginald was distracted, you report. Could he sit with his back to the other kids so as not to see them? Could you read with Tara and at the same time rub Reginald's back or pat his arm, if he likes that? (Some kids don't.)

Dottie

∞

Dear Ellen,

I'm glad that you've decided to be more decisive and clear with the children. They will still like you. Children have exaggerated notions of their own power and are glad to know that an adult will enforce boundaries for them when they can't do it themselves. You know that learner-centered education seeks to teach children to make decisions (one reason for giving so much choice in the classroom) and to take responsibility for their own learning and behavior. All this has to be taught and experienced over time. So it's no contradiction that you are firm and clear and set boundaries.

Thanks for the info on Reginald. Good you noticed some positive things—ability to work in a small group some of the time and to take responsibility some of the time. When you work with him in a small group, can you give him some responsibility, something that he can handle and that you will be able to praise him for later?—perhaps holding the bag with the beans in it, or drawing more papers with set rings on them for his group. Can you find a child who could be his partner for work?

In the classroom can you set up a workspace for one, maybe in a corner where it's quiet and isolated? Other kids may need a quiet spot like that now and then as well. Again, not punishment. Just a recognition that now and then any of us might work better alone. Again you are not punishing, but helping the child. (*You are modifying the environment to fit the child rather than trying to force a child to fit a fixed environment.* The more he succeeds, the better you will like him, and he will like himself better as well.)

Other management issues you raise:

Problems in the coat closet? After the last kid has hung up her coat, close the closet doors. That ends that as a hiding place.

Noise when the chairs are pushed, pulled to bring to the meeting area? Do some demos and return demos, whole class, on how to move a chair. It takes two hands, one under the seat, one on the back of the chair. Lift it a bit off the floor, and then carry it. Set it down quietly. Have a couple of kids demo it and say, "Just right!" Emphasize it for a couple of days. It should help. Amazing, sometimes, the things we have to teach. If it feels overwhelming, just remember it's part of the socializing process that you do legitimately want to teach.

You write that the "place fell apart twice" when you ran the whole day. If only twice, good for you! When I first started teaching I cried every night for a month. I quit three times—thank God for an understanding principal who kept sending me back to try again.

A good way to get a perspective on it, as well as to figure out how to make things work better, is to write down at the end of each day all the things that went well. You'll be surprised at how much did! Then write down what didn't work. See if you can figure out why. Then think of how you might change what you did. If you're like me, after I made new plans I forgot to follow them, and so I cried some more the next night! But it is important to write. It gets better. Look at yourself as you do at the kids; not for total, immediate achievement, but for growth. Allow yourself some failures. Just like the kids, you need to be able to allow yourself to risk, for without risk there is no learning. And risk taking implies the willingness to

accept failure. Then use the failure to change what you're doing and to
move toward learning and success.

Dottie

⟨∞⟩

Dear Johnisha,

I think you handled the boys' argument at the Lego™ table just right. You
acknowledged that they had a disagreement, gave them a chance to figure out
a solution—at the same time offering your support if they felt they needed
it—and assured them you'd be back in five minutes to see how it worked out.
The offer of teacher support gave them security (an adult will help, if needed),
and you gave them a chance to try their wings. Kids need to experiment with
solving social problems, as they do with solving academic ones. Good work.
I agree with you, as you know, about scolding children.

Also, while whole-class discussion about behavior may sometimes be
useful and necessary, my sense is that the doing means more than the talking about it. The issues of focusing and kicking may be a sign that the environment is not right for the kids and needs adjusting. Is there too much
talk, so they get bored, restless, turned off? Should meeting be shorter?
Should focus for meeting be obtained by singing rather than by scolding
and talking? Is there lots of positive reinforcement all day long, so kids feel
good about themselves and the group?

"I like the way Jami is sitting with her legs crossed and her hands in her
lap. I like the way Sonia is quiet so we can start. I like the way Carmen and
Malia share the crayons. How nicely you say 'please' and 'thank you.'
What a good, fast cleanup! Look at that, all the rods and pattern blocks are
picked up!" Little kids love it, and you will create an atmosphere in which
the rewards for doing it right are so palpable that kids will get into it.

Actually, with little kids you can hardly overdo it. I remember in my old
school, where I taught first and second graders and was the only learner-
centered classroom teacher, everyone told me it couldn't be done. That the
kids would break the equipment, that they would steal it. Neither thing
happened. We made a big deal of counting the pencils every day before
lunch, figuring out how many we were missing, and clapping for each child
that found one! A found scissor called for me to dance around the room
with the finder.

Periodically, when the room got messy, we'd do a "treasure hunt." I would hold up the book, or the rods, or the crayons I'd found. Kids would raise their hands if they thought they knew where the object belonged. The rest of us would watch and say "warmer" or "colder" as he headed to the shelves, and we'd clap when the object was replaced. Schmaltzy, but it built the values I wanted for the classroom. Positive reinforcement is the best!

Dottie

∞

Dear Johnisha,

Yes, this is the age when the teeth come out! Any child with a dentist for a parent? Maybe the parent would come to talk, bring an X-ray, demo the toothbrushing. Any pets with teeth? Any jawbones lying around? Lots of possible learnings from looking at teeth.

Dottie

∞

Dear Patrick,

You have picked an interesting child to study. To me he sounds incredibly well-functioning. You could perhaps be more flexible with him—as well as with the others you are working with. Do they really all need to be doing exactly the same thing, even if they are in the same group?

I would think the kids ought to be supported when they have their own ideas. Your child study, for example. When six-year-olds draw before they write, what they are doing is "rehearsing" the story they'll dictate to you later. As they draw, they are making up the story. Us older folk often do this in our heads, or jot a few notes, or make an outline. A six-year-old does it by drawing. If this child wants to dispense with this step and go right to the telling of the story in words, more power to him. *Let him move at his own pace, and in his own way. That's what good teaching is about. Recognizing what the individual child's own way is and providing for it.*

∞

Try to omit the negative in your correcting children. If you praise those who are "doing it right," those who are not will get the point.

If the child doesn't get it, a quiet calling of her name and a simple "It's your turn to listen," or even a silent, negative shake of your head is enough. Otherwise you give reinforcement to negative behavior. You'll get more of it, and your classroom atmosphere, over time, will get nasty. You won't like it.

Dottie

∽

Dear Patrick,

Discussions are hard to do. You'll get better at it! Your description of the book discussion sounded pretty teacher directed and more like a Q-and-A than a real discussion. Here are a few open-ended questions you might try next time to help get at the kids' thinking and the points of connection to the story. These connections might be very different from what you thought they were! "What did you think of the story?" Kid maybe says, "I liked it." You: "Okay. What did you especially like? Tell us more about that. Who else wants to say something about this story?"

If they don't get the point that you think is important, then you might say, "Did anybody notice that there was a problem to be solved in this story?" and go on from there. If you start with the kids' ideas, you will get a much better idea of how and what they think. They'll think more deeply and it will be a real discussion, not a disguised test of comprehension. Incidentally, what a book is about may be different for different readers. Have you not disagreed with a friend about the meaning of a book you've both read? Very legitimate. Also, don't feel you failed if the discussion is very short. Six-year-olds can discuss for an hour if the topic really grips them. Ask yourself if the book was that kind of book.

Another question. I know the point at the moment for the work with pattern blocks is to get the kids to make patterns. That's okay but I wonder if there was time—lots of it—for free exploration with the materials? For kids to build anything they wanted, flat on the table, or rising up? Kids will learn many more things and will build patterns spontaneously. They always do. Pattern making seems to be a necessary human activity!

Take a look in the block area. Do you see any patterns being made there—without teacher direction? Pattern blocks are another one of those wonderful materials that of themselves teach. The teacher has little to do other than set them out. Another advantage to the free work is that after you see patterns emerging, you can say, "Oh. I see a pattern you made. Look. Red, green, red, green or triangle, square, triangle, square." Then you are talking about *his* pattern, and you've only had to name it, not teach it. Much easier!

An extension. Take a "patterns" walk in the neighborhood. Where do you see patterns in the real world? In the arrangement of leaves on a plant? In buildings? A walk inside the school will also turn up patterns. Have the kids look at their own and others' clothing!

In your journal you noted, "Questions were answered by the children with other children agreeing and disagreeing and explaining why." *That* sounds like a discussion.

Dottie

⌘

Dear Patrick,

The "Reading Log Guide" with its guiding questions to the child: How about some open-ended questions? "What would you like to say about this book?" "Do you have a question about this book?"

For the same reasoning that lies behind open-ended questions and activities—to allow the child, to encourage the child to have her own interactions and response to the book, to explore her own ideas, to raise her own questions. Her ideas and questions are her connection to the work. We teachers need to foster the child's sense that *her* ideas are central. That's the way to develop thinkers, instead of robots.

You propose that a first-year teacher use basal readers, even if his school doesn't require it. Why should a first-year teacher use an inferior reading program? You are being exposed to the many ways to begin reading, and hopefully you will grow in your ability to individualize your instruction. Why would you return to the one-size-fits-all method? Remember, it's not only reading "levels" that matter, but interests, attitudes toward literature, learning styles that need to be accounted for. Plus reading in the classroom should be real life. Do you, in your own reading, read out of a reader (other than an anthology), or do you select from numbers of books on a library shelf?

Since you mention first-year teachers, I'm wondering if you are thinking in terms of the management issues when children are free to select their reading materials—how you will teach them to read, and how you will keep track of what they are doing.

Not that hard. You're dealing with little kids right now, so you have an idea of the range of abilities—from nonreader to emerging reader and an occasional fluent one. You'll select and build a wide library from the children's literature to meet this range and from a wide variety of topics to meet the different interests. First day on, you'll teach how to take care of a book (we don't fold over the pages, we don't grab from each other, we want the books to be here for us all year). And you set aside a quiet reading time each day for children to "read," knowing that often means reading the pictures. You'll use the time to model reading by reading your own book quietly and absorbedly or to circulate and read with/to a few children each day so you can assess (and write down) where they are and what clues they use for reading. The rest of early reading instruction you know: reading to children, out-loud choral reading, especially of easily memorizable material including poetry, taking dictation for stories they compose about their drawings, informal reading in the classroom—shelf labels, daily calendar, names, a little phonics, and so on.

It's very hard when we ourselves have been taught traditionally and when such a mystique has been built about reading instruction, to let go and trust that in a classroom where the teacher himself loves reading and enjoys reading to/with kids and lots of opportunity to read is provided for, reading will happen—although not for all kids in the same way and at the same time. The kids for whom there are some major print problems, you will give nonpressure help. Allow yourself to enjoy. Try sitting on the rug with an arm around each of two while you/they read. Just as you would with your own at home.

And speaking about home, you may want to send a book home with each child in a baggie each night for the parent to read to them. A note explaining the procedure goes home first, of course. In my first school, I sent home a form asking who would read with the child—it could be a sibling—and also if the child had a shelf or a shoe box in which to keep his schoolbook). If reading is not a usual at-home experience, parents may need help in thinking how to organize it.

I'm glad your subbing went well and that the children were able to think of pairs of words that went together—including some pairs you hadn't thought of yourself! Isn't that wonderful! Children have such creative ideas.

We teachers need to loosen the blinders we wear so that our thinking expands creatively to all the possibilities that exist and that children offer us.

There was a problem with taking care of the materials? You write, "If it were my classroom I would take away the right to use the materials until they could act like first graders, not babies."

But the teacher's job is precisely to help children learn how to use the materials. How about turning off the light, or whatever quieting signal you use, and say, "I notice something that bothers me. People are letting all the crayons fall on the floor. Raise your hand. What will happen to the crayons if we have them on the floor? Yes! What else might happen to them? Right! So maybe each time you finish using a crayon you should put it back in the container. Would that be a good idea? And if you hear a crayon fall on the floor by mistake, do you think you could pick it up right away? Even if you didn't drop it? Raise your hand if you think you could do both those things? Wonderful! Let's start again. Just table 1 first. Look how nicely they're working. Not a crayon on the floor. Now table 2 . . ."

And walk around praising them for their work with the crayons. Of course, if it were your classroom, you would remind them again next day about the crayons. Lessons are not learned in one day.

I found punishment and denigration of kids ("You act like babies") didn't work. You'll find, I think, that it makes you angry, it makes them angry, and you have a confrontational situation. Use these incidents for teaching—look at them as problems to be solved rather than as discipline issues.

Thanks for sharing everything. An excellent journal.

Dottie

∞

Dear Lisa,

More questions about your literature groups. Good. That means you're constantly evaluating the effectiveness of what you're doing. That's the mark of a good teacher, even though the self-doubt is painful. Keep it up.

I think it's okay for a kid to switch out of a book he doesn't like. Do you always finish a book you start? Just because you thought you would like it at first doesn't necessarily mean you must finish it. On the other hand, a reader does need to give a book a chance, and, yes, you might get lots of requests to switch. Each time you'll have to evaluate if the switch makes sense. So you have options . . . and decisions to make. I'd be inclined to give support to reading on a ways longer rather than just saying yes or no as authority figure.

I agree with you that the literature groups should meet three times weekly. You want to keep the interest high by having the reading moving along. And I'm glad that so many of them did a good job with the response journals. You might want to have a few of the kids read their journals to the whole class, modeling the "how to do it."

You might also want to consider giving the groups the responsibility for managing themselves. I suggest, in order to give support and avoid chaos, you start with a whole-class discussion of possible ways to do a group. See if they have thought of the various mechanisms they'll need (a group leader? how chosen? a way of deciding who reads or comments first?), then give the groups 15 minutes to meet and devise their plan. You circulate among the groups, listen to the plans, ask questions as needed. Then have them start.

The next day or day after—whole class meeting. Each group shares its plan and how the first meeting went. What was easy, hard? What revisions were needed, if any? ("Can you describe how your group decided? Did something go very well? Was something hard to do? How might you change that another time?") That gives some structure to the process of self-organization without taking away the possibility of kids' trying out different methods and choosing among multiple possibilities. As you circulate during succeeding days, you'll be evaluating how the groups are doing. Periodically you may want another whole class session on how things are working. *In this way you are giving the same thoughtful attention and guidance to the learning of how to learn (in this case, how to run a group) as you would to any other subject matter.*

Learning how to work productively in a group is a skill worth learning. It is of lifelong use. Consider the time spent on this not as taking away from the reading but as part of your plan of teaching. Learning how to do anything requires doing it, thinking about it, discussing it, revising it, trying again, and so on.

Re: a parent conference for the child who is too social. At the meeting ask the child how she thinks the problem could be solved. Should she sit alone? Should she decide (with you) each day how much she'll accomplish, a sort of contract? How does she think you might help her? How can her mother help? Make the plan realistic. If the child fools around all the time, maybe set a small goal for the first plan. Perhaps sitting alone, working quietly, just during writing. Or sitting with a friend but working quietly, just for writing. It is more important that the child succeed at this point than that she accomplish a lot. Success builds on success. Don't forget to write down the plan, read it to the conference, have everyone agree and sign it and then set a date for a follow-up conference.

Dottie

ℂ

Dear Lisa,

I'm glad that some of what you see is beginning to become clearer to you. You are right in noting that M. J.'s ability as an artist is valued by others. When that happens she can value it, too, and feel good about herself, especially in view of the difficulties she has with print learning.

It is important to understand that the recognition and valuing of abilities besides those of print learning has importance not only for issues of the child's self-esteem. These abilities may be this child's entry to many fields of learning.

For M. J. as an artist, her ability to draw and paint and build may be a pathway into science, for instance. In her artist's work she must deal with issues of balance, perspective, lines, characteristics of different materials: paper, clay, wood, kinds of paint. The math of scale. Painting can lead to the science skill of close observation. Does the sky end at a line across a landscape? When you look at a painting, how does an artist tell you her story? Is a thing three-dimensional? How has the artist told you that? What's the weather? What's the mood? What's the century like in which she painted? How can you tell from a picture? Wouldn't art museum trips be great here? How do you know a storm is coming, a wind is blowing?

When you recognize a child's ability and provide for it in your classroom, you are providing a pathway from the child's interest and strength to the wider body of knowledge a well-educated person should have.

Dottie

ℂ

Dear Lisa,

You ask about the kids' behavior. Where does it come from? It comes off
the street, out of the newspapers, on the TV, out of our adult world. Violence is in their lives. Their parents tell them, "Be tough. If he hits you, hit
him back." They see it as survival—and honor! The school therefore has to
work forever to establish its own culture.

Each classroom, each teacher, has to do it in his own room. It can be
done! Even if not perfectly each and every day. The classroom must be a
safe place and an accepting one for everyone, including for the children
who fight. We have to be firm, but not angry. We often have to teach them
the very words that keep the classroom comfortable and have them practice
using those words. Blame and punishment don't work. Acceptance of the
legitimacy of feelings is important; the teaching and reteaching of acceptable behavior must be part of the curriculum.

So how to do it? There are lots of techniques. First of all, teachers have to
model the desirable behavior themselves! While teachers don't physically
fight with each other, students need to see that teachers do talk together,
laugh together, discuss and argue, and remain colleagues. Teachers also have
to model the give-and-take behavior with their own students. The authoritarian approach sends the message, "You have to do it my way, because I am
bigger than you!" which carries the message to the kids that to get what you
want, you need to show the other person that you are "bigger." So teacher
modeling with other teachers and with the kids is the first step.

As you know, the very first day of school, and as often as needed thereafter, build the rules with the kids: We're all here to learn and to help each
other learn. Therefore, we must respect each other. In this school, we
respect each other's bodies. We don't fight. We respect each other's feelings.
We don't call names. We respect each other's work, so we don't scribble on
each other's papers or tear up each other's projects. Or the alternative
wording, "Everyone has a right to feel safe and to learn. Did this action
make people feel safe? Did it help them learn?"

So what do you do if someone bothers you? Explore the possibilities
with the kids. They'll usually start off with, "Tell the teacher." I say, "Yes,
you could do that, but what things could you do before you come to tell
me?" Eventually we work out a step-by-step procedure. First, tell the person bothering you to stop what she's doing. Sometimes people don't realize
what they're doing upsets you. They say, "I was just playing." If the person

*Figure 3.5 Conflict resolution. "You must talk to each other, not to me.
How will you solve that?" The teacher requires the children to try to
solve their conflict; she stands by.*

doesn't stop, try telling her once more. After that, you have options. These
include walking away (very hard for kids to do!), finding a compromise or
doing it her way since she cares so much (e.g., she wants the same chair you
do. Does it really matter?). I say, "If that doesn't work, come to me."

In terms of your responses, if someone hits another person, stop it at once.
"Oh, no. We don't do that in this school." And follow with a reminder,
"What could you have done instead? Good remembering. That's the way!"

When you get, as you surely will, "My mother told me if someone hits
me I should hit him back," respond, "That's fine. If your mother wants you
to hit back when you are at home or on the street, that's fine. But in school
we do it this way." Such a response does not put you and the parent on
opposite sides of the fence—very important. And kids can accept different
behaviors as being appropriate to different places. After all, you can walk
around your apartment in your bathrobe, that's fine, but you wouldn't
wear it to work. Same deal. Each behavior has its appropriate place. Kids
can deal with it.

Where you have ongoing problems, you may want to do some minilessons via role-play. I used to have a lot of fun being the "bad" kid, and giving

the children a chance to role-play the situation with me for the class. There are lots of good curriculums around conflict resolution. Look at Educators for Social Responsibility—they have prepared a lot of stuff.[7] I'm sure we'll talk more about this as the semester proceeds.

Dottie

⚊

Dear Lisa,

You raise more questions about "discipline." Don't tell a kid to get in line three times. Tell her once, and then say, "I guess you're not ready. Go back in the room. I'll call you later, when I think you're ready." And don't argue about it or give into, "Please, may I have a second chance." The answer to that is, "Of course, in a few minutes. Go back in the room until I call you."

I know this is easy for me to say, and hard to do! I remember my first years of teaching in my old school. The mark of a good teacher was the straightness and quietness of her hall lines! I simply couldn't do it and finally gave up trying. But after awhile I began to figure out the techniques. It will come!

Meanwhile try all the techniques. Walk backwards and look at them. Stop periodically and wait in silence. Silently motion out a few well-behaved kids and whisper to them to go on to lunch without you. Hold the rest. Have dependable line leaders and instruct them to stop at every stair landing. You stand and monitor the whole line as it passes you, and then tell the leaders to move on. If it's just a couple of unruly ones, you can tell them to go down with another class (clear this with that teacher first), or do as I did and forget it for now. Unruly lines are embarrassing, but not the core of teaching.

Dottie

⚊

CHAPTER 4

Why Kids Work:
The Role of Choice and Structure ∽
An Environment Where
Questions Can Happen ∽
Discipline, Assessment,
Parents as Partners

∽

I am amazed at how they really seem connected to the work. They were eager to read their interviews to the class...

Rebecca

I liked how the teacher went through and asked each child what they were going to do. She marked it down and then after project time they needed to go to their journals and write what they did that day. Each child knew what was expected of him. Also during project time the teacher interviewed a child to see what he was working on and what his thoughts were...

Lisa

Before they start a project they need to discuss what they're going to do, then they have to write about how it is going, and, lastly, they critique it...

Sam

While the children seem to have a lot of freedom, they seemed to have a real sense of responsibility and ownership in the work they do. Those who were good at the computers wanted to help everyone else with the computers. Those good at poetry would listen to each other's work, make suggestions and compliment . . .

Rebecca

For some of the projects I still have some questions about what they are learning. For example, making a papier-maché vase. Where does the academia come in? Also, one child who was making a city, while he drew a floor plan first, he never used a ruler to measure anything. This was a point the teacher brought up in the interview. I am a little confused about when the children are learning science and social studies . . .

Lisa

It works perfectly with young children. There is so much room for the children to explore different things. They also seem to really gain a sense of individuality and independence. They also really communicate with each other, especially if someone did something they did not like or they wanted something that no one else had. I am beginning to get the feeling that this type of approach is great for younger children but is not as productive for older ones . . .

Lisa

- ☯ "The having of wonderful ideas"
- ☯ Projects as science, history, and social studies
- ☯ Model making re-creates experience
- ☯ Experiencing and constructing lead to new questions
- ☯ Relevance to older children
- ☯ Experiencing made age appropriate
- ☯ Creating an environment where questions can happen
- ☯ Discipline again—punishment versus consequence
- ☯ Conflict and resolution as "teachable moments"
- ☯ When meetings don't work
- ☯ Reading partners
- ☯ Writing workshop
- ☯ Ending a discussion

Dear Lisa,

I'm glad you liked the other upper-grade room you visited and I'm pleased that you were able to know what it was that you were seeing, including the "subject matter"—and recognizing the kind of management techniques that make all this individualized learning happen.

Re: science and social studies as "subjects." As you saw, there was a lot of science going on in many of the projects, although maybe not the same science for all the kids at the same time. Does that matter? If you feel kids must have a certain science or social studies experience, you could plan for that as a class unit. Just be sure you've allowed for different interests and different pathways to the knowledge for the different kids in your room. This teacher feels it more important to follow the individual child's passion. Be sure to read that article I gave you, Eleanor Duckworth's "The Having of Wonderful Ideas."[8] It will help you think about this teacher's approach.

I can imagine social studies happening out of those morning meeting discussions this teacher leads (and prepares for!). Pick topics kids might feel passionate about—women's rights, kid's rights, environmental issues, the high school and college students' demonstrations against school budget cuts. You don't take a position on any of these issues. Your job is to help them see different points of view, to examine evidence, perhaps to do some research for further discussion. All these topics could easily lead to the societal issues, which are social studies.

And if you feel they need some history as history, be sure to put in your unit lots of hands-on activity. If you do "Early Immigrants," get a sheep's wool, wash it, comb it, card it, spin it, weave it. Make a quilt. Make dyes from natural materials, dye cloth, make butter, dry fruits, make models, dress dolls—live the time.

Integrated curriculum is wonderful! You saw some kids making paper. Paper involves science. It can also involve art and history! Think of papermaking out of scrap paper, to recycling, to forestry practices, the social studies of the forces pro and con cutting the forests, hemp as a substitute for trees in paper (science), old ways of papermaking, papyrus, museum trip to look at parchment and illuminated manuscripts from medieval times (history). See if there's an exhibit of art papers. There's no end to it, once you allow your imagination to run.

Look at all the science that you saw! The death of the fish in Sara's room led to dissection and to an examination of a collection of bones from a variety of animals. Some other thing that grew out of mixing led a group to work with molasses, water, other kitchen substances in test tubes. Look at the kids' involvement! That means learning is happening! Because it's their interests, their ideas being pursued.

Science doesn't have to be in 45-minute periods, two days a week! In fact, it shouldn't be—science should be an ongoing daily experience, but more on that later. A teacher that wants science to happen needs to think about what to put in his room so that kids have something to ask questions about! *The teacher's job is to set up an environment that encourages the child to ask her own science questions—these may be different child to child—and then to help the child seek answers and discover that there are more questions to ask.* Look how splendidly Win's trip to the Harlem Meer worked. The trip set up the environment in which science questions could happen and also allowed for different children to have different questions, depending on their individual connection to the common experience. Did Win know in advance what those questions would be? Not exactly, but she knew what some of the possibilities were and had decided in advance that the possibilities would be worth studying. She was also willing for the kids to explore other possibilities that she might not have thought of.

Anticipating the *possibilities*, Win brought along some plastic (not glass) containers and small nets for collecting water samples and small creatures.

And then the unexpected happened. A turtle! A little one. The question the kids had—"Does such a turtle belong in this body of water?" And the rest you saw. Again, the teacher's role was to encourage pursuit of the questions, and having equipment on hand (water tank, hand magnifier) so that some of the questions could be pursued then and there.

We believe this kind of science knowledge, generated by exploration, does all those good things of creating kids who have confidence in the legitimacy of their own questions, stimulates curiosity, spurs scientific thinking, and helps the child hold onto some of the facts. Are these the facts of the prescribed curriculum? Maybe yes, maybe no. Chances are, over the years in the school most of what's prescribed gets learned, and other stuff besides.

Dottie

☙

Dear Martha,

It is hard to know where to end a discussion—weighing the class's and your need to move on with a lesson or activity as opposed to listening to each child's ideas. A few techniques that might help.

Acknowledge the number of hands that are up. "I see how many of you have ideas, but we need to move on, so I'll call on two people, and try to get the rest of you another time." Or if there's an urge on everybody's part to respond to the book acknowledge that and talk about the one page, scrap the plan to read the whole book at one sitting, and spread it over several days.

Re: the excitement and noise from lunch and recess. It's often very hard for kids to calm down! Do you line them up outside your room before you bring them in? Sometimes a good and necessary thing to do. Let a few in at a time, with a reminder of what the next activity is. It will help them to slow down and focus. Is there an afternoon rest or quiet time? Quiet music and resting are great.

Dottie

⌒

Dear Lisa,

You ask how long project time should be and how often it should happen. That time, when children are building and making things, should be long enough that real work can get done and that the work maintains a forward motion. If the time allotted is not long enough, you lose the work-impelling enthusiasm that you want. At the same time, you don't want the time so long that kids get tired and slack off. As always, you'll take your cues from the kids. You'll watch and listen, and then decide.

For you, I think, there's another issue, as yet unresolved. It's how you see or don't see the project work as integral, or not integral, to learning (in all areas we've talked about—academic, personal, social). Project time is not just for kids to have choices of fun things to do so they can't complain about the rest of the day. It's an issue of how children learn best.

Here you need to refer back to Dewey and how he viewed "experiencing" in terms of learning and intellectual growth. Also reread the article by Debbie Meier on why we make so many models at CPE (see Appendix F). Remember her idea that recreating an experience by making a model of it helps us to understand that experience better. How does a building really look? Are roofs always pointed? (Think of how little kids paint houses—all with pointed roofs and lollipop trees next to the house! Even when they live in New York City.) So how do houses really look? If it's a brick house, are the bricks in columns with vertical lines of mortar between them? What holds a building up? How does an elevator work? Where are windows placed? Do I need a ramp to get cars into my model garage? Is the sky a thin blue line at the top of my view? (Think of the kids' paintings again!) Where does the sky end? Is water always blue? What other colors do you see in it? What does the sky look like in a storm? How do you know where the sun is shining when you look at an object? How about bridges and arches? Why don't the stones fall out?

Might I as builder or painter need to do some research—look at some books, visit a museum, an architect's office?

As teacher, can you see the possibilities for history, social studies, science? The Romans had astounding building machines. And think what a building project the pyramids were! Take a look at Macaulay's books.[9] He's got one on pyramids, one on the Romans, one on how machines work, and one on the city sewer system!

How things look and how they work and the history of them (which is the world around us) becomes relevant. Therefore, there's a greater chance for learning to take place. It grows out of a child's experience and interest. When the child needs the information for his model or painting, he's more likely to learn it and learn it in a meaningful way. Project time to be useful should be thought of as one of those marvelously fruitful times when a child gets a chance to ask his own question, construct something around it, do his research, while the teacher encourages exploration and looks for ways to deepen the learning. Additionally, it is during this process of experiencing and constructing that new questions arise for the child, questions that otherwise might not occur. These questions form the basis for new learnings. Project time is not separate from the rest of the day nor a sop to "He's only a child." Let him do a child's thing and have fun. It's a dignified time to do dignified work.

One last note. At our lunch meeting this week, Sam and Rebecca commented on the children's investment in their work, their sense of ownership of it, their seriousness about helping each other. Might there be a connection between these things and the fact that the children have so much choice about what they study and how they study it?

You ask, "How long should cleanup take?" After project time, about 10 minutes. Some kinds of work, like painting, might need a little longer. You can solve that by going quietly to the painting group 5 minutes earlier to tell them to start. If you've given the 5-minute warning to cleanup that gives kids

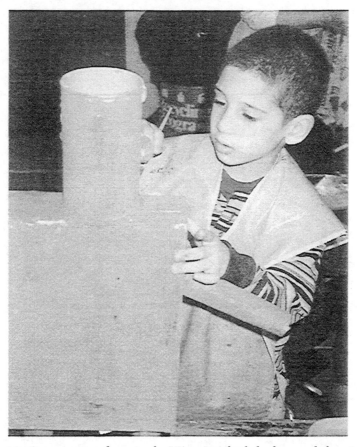

Figure 4.1 Construction from junk. "First I picked the box and then I picked some legs and then some arms and then I tried to pick some eyes. Then I paint the legs. Then I paint the box. Then I paint the arms, the nose, the cheeks, and the eyes. I think in my brain that I wanted to make a robot."

a chance to wind down and let go of their work, it will be easier for them. Some kids really do hate to stop, but if they must, help them by reminding them they can work again on their project tomorrow. Circulate, if you need to, to see that cleanup moves along. Give positive reinforcement for good cleaning up! Occasionally you might need to tell a few kids to skip recess and return to cleanup, but avoid that if you can. You need recess, too.

Dottie

Figure 4.2

Dear Lisa,

You note that when you went to the district science fair, some of the science projects seemed to have had more put into the visual than into the study aspect for the exhibit. Probably right. As teacher, you have to make your teacher judgments. How deep is the child's interest in this project? Is this child capable of deeper study, and should I therefore insist on more research? Is this as far as this child can go? Is the visual an important learning and emotional connection for this child? Clearly, you'll make different decisions for different children.

I started the bottom. I put the thing on the bottom. I put two boxes in the middle. I put two boxes on the side. I put glue on it. Then I put the top two. I put glue on the bottom of the 7th and 8th boxes and I put 1 box on top. I put the other one box on top. Then I put paper towel on top. Then I started to cut the star and I glue it and stick to the paper towel. Then I paint it gray and black for the windows (xx

Figure 4.3

I'm glad you liked Yvette's pre-K class. Yes, it's easy to see how a learner-centered classroom encourages exploration and independence in little ones. The connection with the environment—the sand, water, paint, blocks—so obvious! And so direct! The materials really teach! But note that Yvette knew what questions little ones might have (even if they don't ask in words) *provided she has created an environment that suggests the questions.* That's why there's wet sand and dry sand, sieves, and cookie tins in each.

(Differences in the nature of wet/dry sand will be revealed with sieves and cookie tins.) That's why the water table has containers of different sizes and shapes, a water wheel, and a pump. (Not just sink and float, is it?) Can you think of the questions that might be asked? And the science that's being experienced? Try "playing" with these materials yourself, at home if not at school. What do you learn? What questions occur?

But back to the original point. The learning from the environment is easy to see in a learner-centered classroom for little ones. It's harder to see with older kids, in large part because we are so used to thinking in terms of teacher-directed and paper-pencil-and-textbook learning as being "real school" and "real learning"; play is okay for little ones, but now we are big!

We forget that learning takes place in the same way—through experiencing—with older kids (and even with adults)! With older kids, we can deepen their experiencing because they can read, they can conceptualize abstractly to a greater extent—but it has to be conceptualizing and abstracting that begins with experiencing.

The other harder part is that you probably cannot put out sand and water and expect the materials to carry the learning on. Interest might not last because, after all, they're not five-year-olds, and after a few days of revisiting their five-year-oldness with the sand and water, they'll get bored. So you, the teacher, have to think, "How do I set up the sand and water experience so that it's age appropriate?" Maybe it's Win's trip to the Meer and the bringing back of water samples and the use of a microscope to study the water creatures.

Maybe it's a whole water curriculum that explores in depth such things as river currents, waves, land erosion, islands, deltas, dams, floods, filtration, water pollution, estuaries—all of this in a curriculum that begins in your classroom sand-water table. This is a curriculum in which these water phenomena can be created, seen, experienced—and then built on with books and trips, expanded research, and written reports. You'll be glad to know you don't have to invent this curriculum. There are plenty of water curriculums on hand that you can select from.

Maybe it's not kindergarten-size blocks (although it could be). Maybe it's Lego™ for building and Lego™-computer. Maybe it's foam board and glue—instead of blocks—and the buildings made to scale. As Debbie has said, we need to put the kindergarten into the upper grades. I think this may be what she meant.

Dottie

⋍

Figure 4.4 First we made some model animals. Then we decided to make a house for them. We made the bunk bed first. We put it on a slant so we could slide right down the stairs! First Kelsey wanted a big house. Then we decided for two floors 'cause we could have a yard. The chimney thing could be a rocket. We made a rough draft of the refrigerator. We're going to make a second draft. That means do it all over again, a different way. When are we going to make the alarm? Chelsea said, "Make it last, so we don't get paint on it." We wanted the house pink and blue. I said, "Let's not fight about it. Let's solve this thing. We could do stripes, and we each have our colors!"

Dear Lisa,

You made good learning use of all your week's experiences. Good for you! You don't waste a minute!

Re: grams and meters. Probably they should know it by this time. What sorts of classroom experiences could you plan so they would know meters and know grams and when to use each? No formal lesson needed, except perhaps as a summing up at some point or as a reminder to them that they do know.

Re: keeping the kids from recess who didn't do their math. I agree with you that this time should have been used to do the math—including those who left the homework at home!

They need to do it again—right now! The reason they were allowed to read, write, or whatever instead, I would guess, is that the teacher viewed the loss of recess as punishment instead of consequence—which is not a semantic difference. Math needed to be ready that day. If not done at home, needed to be done during the school day. The only part of the school day not already programmed for something else is recess; therefore that becomes math time. Stay away from punishment. It doesn't work. Stay with consequence. It makes sense to kids, and the logic of it helps avoid the build up of anger that happens when it's punishment—the strong over the weak.

*Figure 4.5 Second/third graders make a model of the school building. A trip out-
side to sketch and measure was step 1. But the translation from drawing to model
proved hard. They needed to work with blocks or Lego™ so they could move the
building parts around. Here they check the accuracy of their Lego™ model by
looking out the window. The final model, made of cardboard and papier-mâché,
included the courtyard with its mural, the several entrances, and the recess yard.*

Sounds like you used conflict resolution techniques well with the angry
kids. This method really helps children learn good ways to behave with
each other as individuals and how to work comfortably in a group. Just
about everything that happens in a classroom can be used to teach—if we
recognize our opportunities! To do that, we have to drop punishment and
authority as major modes of relating to kids. These are blinders that prevent
us from recognizing the teachable moments.

Dottie

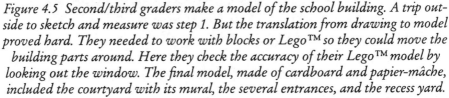

Figure 4.6 Fifth/sixth grader Krystal built her dream house with "lots of bedrooms so lots of kids can stay over." She included a hot tub, a gym, an office, and an exercise room. Floor plans accompany her model.

Dear Sam,

Thanks for your good journal. I made a few short comments in the margins, mostly agreeing with your concerns!

No, children should not get up and walk around or hold private conversations during group discussions. No, they should not be noisy in the hallways.

How to deal with kids who don't come to meeting or who disrupt it or who talk through it? One should not stop a meeting over and over for individual kids, so you have to analyze why it's happening. Then you will know what to do, although what you do may not be the same each time or the same for each kid.

Some basic questions:

Is the subject matter and its presentation of interest or appropriate to the group? Meetings first thing in the morning are usually used to organize the day's events, choosing projects, sometimes a brief minilesson. Meetings after project time usually are for sharing of learnings and as transition to a different activity. Meeting at the end of the day provides closure. I used to read to the class, a quiet coming together before saying good-bye. Is there a signal to come to meeting that has been practiced and is understood by the group, and is it a relatively quiet one so that the atmosphere is quiet? Has a 5-minute warning to "finish up your work—meeting is coming" been given, so kids can more easily wind down and switch gears?

Are there some kids you can anticipate having a hard time at meeting, and have you anticipatorily (if there is such a word) provided for them?—seating them by you so you can give them a gentle pat when they get restless, separating them from their chatty friends, excusing them totally from meeting to read or write alone (this only after discussion in advance with the child and only for kids who can hardly ever handle a large group.) More about this another time.

Do the kids need help in knowing how to be quiet? With eight- and nine-year-olds I often had to start meeting with "Check your feet. They should be on the floor in front of you. Check your hands. They should be in your lap. Check your mouth. It should be quiet. Now find the quiet place inside of you." Then after a few moments of this yoga-like relaxing silence, I'd say, "Good. You look terrific. We can start."

Once meeting starts, there should be no interruptions for behaviors. Your quiet voice sets the tone. Reminders to raise hands are okay. Kids acting silly—either control them with a silent stare, or shake your head, or in a very quiet voice, say, "Stephen, leave us, please. Sit at [some place he can hear the discussion but not disturb it]."

Other possibilities, always with a quiet voice, "If your neighbor is talking, help her by putting your finger on your mouth." You don't want kids to "help" you saying "Shhh" or "Be quiet." That only adds to the noise.

The cooking sounds like fun. Maybe the kids would now like to write down the recipe and copy it to go home so everyone can try it (writing, reading).

I'm glad, too, that your math group is going well. Remember to praise for good behaviors! Keep me informed of how it goes.

Dottie

⚮

Dear Sam,

Thanks for the good journal, again!

We talked today about what to do with the child who has poor reading skills and whines about baby books. Suggest he take the hard book home; perhaps an older sibling or parent will help him read it. I never liked to say to a child, "That book is too hard for you"—in quite that way. Better to say, "That's a good book you picked. Would you like to take it home tonight?

For now, let's find a book you can read all by yourself." And then I'd help him pick one.

Other things you can do. First of all, when I started at the beginning of the year, I read with each child individually—just briefly—and talked with him about his interests. I wrote it down in my teacher's reading book. That gave me a beginning assessment of approximately where that child was with his reading and what his interests were. Then I could kind of group the kids— tentatively—into those who were fluent and didn't need my help, those who seemed about right (not fluent but probably only needing to do lots of reading to become so), and those who seemed to need a lot of special attention.

Next I set up reading partners for that special group, usually from someone in that middle group. The fluent readers, I found, often became too impatient to be helpers and were really into reading fast and not being interrupted. Also I didn't want it to seem too much a "teacher-student" relationship. I did want it to be more a partnership. In setting up these partnerships, I always checked with both kids to see if they were willing. Each reading period the partners would read together for 10 minutes, and then each read alone (or with me, individually) for the rest of the time. That gave individualized help to the child needing help and the more advanced child still had time to read his own stuff.

Should you have lots of struggling readers, you'll still partner kids to help each other, and you'll do more choral reading so lots of kids are reading together.

Assessment, then reading partners. Try these ideas as well: (1) Have a listening corner with books on tape so the child can hear the book and follow the print with her eyes. (2) Find some simple plays for reading/practicing parts, and have the small group, when they're ready, read or act the play for the class. (3) Do some group poetry reading or dramatic reading with solo and chorus parts. (4) Make an arrangement with the pre-K, K, or first grade teacher to have a few of your kids read to individual kids in his room. Have your kids practice reading "easy books" so that they can read them to the little kids. This makes "easy books" much more acceptable to older kids as reading material. And, of course, for kids with major reading problems, ask the resource room teacher for help in analyzing and setting up a reading approach for each.

You ask—do learner-centered classroom teachers have to work harder than traditional teachers? Mostly they have to work differently.

Dottie

∞

Dear Sam,

You ask for a method to make writing time more fruitful. Beth described
Win's writing workshop for us at lunch the other day. Writing workshop
worked reasonably well for me, too. Here's how I did the mechanics of it. I
found that most kids who were used to choosing their own writing subjects
didn't need help to think of something to write about. So I usually started
each writing time by asking the group to raise hands if they knew what
they'd write about. Those I excused from the meeting to get to work, to
write silently. The others I kept for guidance. Sometimes that small remain-
ing group would brainstorm together. Other times, I gave each 5 minutes
with a friend to brainstorm. After five minutes I'd say, "Conferencing time
is over," and they'd start writing. After 5 minutes, still no idea, I'd say,
"Write about something that happened at home last night or in the morning
or before you came to school, no matter how dumb it seems to be, because
in the act of writing the idea will come."

At this age of eight or nine, no one needs to draw first. Drawing first as a
way of "rehearsing" and developing the story idea is appropriate for pre-K,
K, first, and maybe a few second graders. But by this age writing (the
mechanics of it) and familiarity with story are sufficient so that they can
start with writing. If they don't like what they write, they can scratch it out.
I used to encourage that, in fact, to legitimize the idea of "drafts" and cor-
rections and changing of minds, and as a way to avoid wasting paper. Kids
love a clean sheet of paper and will throw out a whole page if they write
two words they don't like! Trees, you know. We don't do that!

After I saw that everyone had started, I began individual conferences,
first with those who had read their work to the class the day before and had
received critiques and ideas—to remind them of what those ideas were and
to ask which they planned to use and where they expected to make changes.
Then, if there was time left, I did one or two other conferences, trying, over
time, to talk periodically with each child. There never seemed to be enough
time. And after I stopped taking their writing home to comment on it at
night, I tried to comfort myself by saying that the group conferencing perhaps did most of the job.

So, after silent writing (maybe 30 to 40 minutes), we gathered again, and
two or three children shared their writing with the class for group critique.

Once kids get pretty good at critiquing—that is, recognizing what questions to ask the author to help him think about his story—you may be able to
increase the critiquing by forming three or four critiquing groups meeting
simultaneously. More kids get to read and receive critiquing help that way.

I haven't dealt here with the content of writing workshop, just with the mechanics. As you know, you can and should relate literature to it; use the books kids are reading for examples of good "opening sentences" and other techniques, you can do minilessons and "exercises" where you think they'd be helpful, and so on. And, when you do literature groups, you'll want to look at these books in part for a discovery of the author's craft—how he or she builds suspense, interest, mood, and so on. Reading and writing are related, and the learning can be integrated so naturally.

Dottie

☙

CHAPTER 5

Playgrounds ∾
Homeless Study ∾
Thoughts on Assessment, Authority,
Writing, and Grammar

∾

Last week we visited our first playground. The kids observed and wrote in their notebooks for about 20 minutes before they played. They came up with ideas we adults had not even thought of! One was whether the weight or height of the person coming down the slide had anything to do with the speed of descent. The children discussed this for quite awhile. They decided to experiment by using blocks to create a ramp and sending down one solo block and then several blocks taped together.

Today, the kids got into measuring the tall equipment. They were so creative! Alix asked James to stay on top of the sliding pole while she stood against the bottom. Maritza estimated that another person might fit between Alix's head and James' feet, so that it made three persons altogether. David counted the boards on the bridge. There were seventy-seven. Each was as wide as Monty's feet. Then they multiplied . . .

Rebecca

∾   Playground study

∾   Homeless unit as social studies

∾   Developmental issues in writing

∾   Assessment, evaluation, record keeping, portfolios

∾   Family conference

∾   Cats and dogs

77

- Teacher role in a discussion
- Activity curriculum for youngers and olders
- The role of choice—does it make a difference in learning?
- Maximizing the work output by knowing each kid
- Parents as partners
- Writing conventions

Dear Rebecca,

The playground study is so rich already!

The ideas for experimenting with weight/height on the slide are great. Another question: Might the incline affect speed? If they don't think of it themselves, you could ask, "Might anything other than the person's height/ weight affect the speed? What do you think? How might you test it? I wonder what a curve on a slide might do. What about the surface? If it were sandpapery would that matter?"

Other extensions: roller coasters. Speed going down affecting speed going up? Try marble chutes in the block area. And after lots of their inventing experiments, some books.

Dottie

∞

Dear Martha,

You wrote about a day when nothing worked, when the kids were doing their own thing, and nothing you did could change it. It happens to all teachers. Sometimes even throughout the school. Something in the air? We never know what causes such "off" days. Write it off. Forget it. Other days are coming. And there's plenty of time to teach what needs to be taught.

Dottie

∞

Dear Sam,

I'm glad the homeless unit got off to such a good start. It sounds as if you are having more and more successes. I'm looking forward to seeing your unit plan, particularly the semantic map, and the individual pieces—or lessons—that you plan.

I like your idea of a reflective journal kept by the kids and your plan to take these journals home with you for dialoguing with the kids, a fine idea, one that might be made even better if you had more class discussions, especially around questions that come up in their journals. Two reasons: (1) a group discussion is a group dialogue—more ideas may come out, more points of view, things that you as teacher and adult may not even have thought of! Children get to evaluate their thoughts in terms of the responses of many people, not just the teacher's. Then, hopefully, what they write will be even more thoughtful. (2) Since in our kind of teaching we want teachers to step back as much as possible, replacing themselves with the children's own resources—if the dialogue is the group's (with the teacher facilitating the discussion by asking "What do you think? Could you explain that a little more? Tell us more about that. Have you information about that? Who has a different idea? Wait, let's discuss this last idea a little more, and then we'll get to your point . . . "), this makes response more children sourced and less teacher sourced.

It's less between you and them directly and more between them and them.

Kids do love it, however, when teachers write to them personally in their journals, and, of course, they will read the teacher's comments, so you do get more reading—an advantage. Practical matter—it's a lot of work—after school to read twenty-five journals and respond to them individually. A decision for you!

Dottie

⌘

Dear Sam,

I know your homeless unit is primarily to meet the assignment for a reading class, but it's a great social studies unit as well. Have you made plans to visit a homeless shelter or soup kitchen or to interview politicians or people who work with and for the homeless? All sorts of possibilities. If you decide to do it, let's talk about how.

Also use the newspapers. A great opportunity to have kids see the newspaper as a source for information. Pull articles from the papers yourself. Paraphrase if the reading is too hard and use the article to start a discussion. You might get some research projects out of it, where information is incomplete or different viewpoints are put forth. Newspapers are hard for eight- and nine-year-olds, but you could have them cut out articles, have their parents read the articles to them, and have them interview their parents for additional information on the topic. Then they can bring the article and the discussion results to the class. Interviewing parents is an excellent way for kids to learn interview skills. I found, also, that while some parents felt embarrassed by not knowing as much as they thought they should about a topic, they were flattered and liked the participation they felt in their child's learning.

A classroom management idea. If you want kids to write after a discussion, you don't have to excuse them to go to table and come back again. You could have them bring their journals and pencils and have them write while seated in the group. Have a couple of sharpened extra pencils on hand! This method saves some time and may help the focus. Just one alternative in your arsenal of methods.

The writing feedback issue that you mention: There are developmental issues, natural progressions in children's writings. Eights and nines tend to write linearly. "This happened first, this second, this third. I got up in the morning. Then I ate breakfast. Then I went to school." The idea of maybe starting in the middle and doing flashbacks, or picking one item from the list, elaborating and making the whole piece around it is beyond a lot of them. No matter how well your writing workshop goes, no matter how well you conference, no matter how you force a well-written final draft—they will still return to the linear list! A revision for many of them will merely be the rewording of that first item on the list, or of the last one.

Which doesn't mean that critiquing, examining, and discussing literature and conferencing are a waste of time. They're not. Some kids will be able to do it; for the others, you're helping lay the groundwork for when they are developmentally able. Incidentally, even when my eights and nines didn't change the way they wrote they did get very good at critiquing and recognizing author techniques!

You may want to look at some of the literature-based reading/writing programs. Their way might work better than mine did.

Re: math teaching. I suspect even in your little group there are different levels of understanding of the concept. Can you make the lesson more flexible so that the more able can do something with what they know while you work with the others?

Yes, the small size of the school does foster a sense of belonging—and safety for the kids. Very important. We need to have small schools at all age levels. Kids need to know and be known in the school community.

When you get a new kid in the class, you might want to ask someone to be her buddy—to see that she gets to lunch and recess and back again, to understand what we do in the room and how we do it. Sometimes older kids' teachers and younger kids' teachers have arranged buddy systems for their entire rooms—for one-on-one reading to/with, on a two-days-a-week basis, for example. More community and more individualized instruction, too!

Dottie

∞

Dear Sam,

Glad your homeless unit continues to go well!

About the filming on the street. I can't believe that that experience should upset a whole class all day! No way! Were they able to talk at morning meeting about the filming? A good opportunity to grab something of immediate interest for possible learning. Share their knowledge, make a list of questions they have about filming. Maybe the start of a mini-unit, including interviewing some member of the crew, or a filmmaker, a chance to write a script of their own, videotape the acting of it? You can see the possibilities for science, art, reading, writing, and research skills. It need not get in the way of your homeless unit and is one of those marvelous real-life events that may spur learning!

Maybe only a small group wants to do it, maybe you'll give it a couple days a week, maybe you'll use the immediate situation just to list the knowledge and the questions and put the investigation off for a little while. You'll need time, anyway, to scout resources. So use the current filming event as a starter, have the discussion, and then say, "Okay, now it's time to . . . " and on to the next activity. And—begin! That's it.

Re: the moaning and groaning when you give a "must do" assignment. Ignore it. It will stop without the negative reinforcement that your trying to appease them gives. Just give the assignment, and don't argue about it.

Dottie

∞

Dear Sam,

I agree with all your journal comments! Yes, celebrating differences should be each and every day and it can be differences in art ability, drama ability, construction ability, social problem-solving ability. It's not fake, either, to celebrate these differences. These abilities are needed for a good full life. *Our problem often is that we separate out "school learning" from all the rest of real living and give praise in school only for "school learning," that narrowly defined area of functioning, in spite of the fact that school learning really depends on so much other stuff that is often disregarded or overlooked.* Assessment, evaluation, and measurement. Not so hard. A big deal is made out of it. Trust yourself, your ability to look at a kid working and to assess from your observations her interests, her skills—academic and social. Look for her strengths and for those things she might need help with. Your observations will be as scientific and as valid as any test measures. Look at the Primary Language Record as one way to keep track. And do keep track—informally, through watching/listening, during reading/writing conferences, through watching math now and then— and write it down. This kind of ongoing record keeping is essential; makes it possible to have different projects going simultaneously and for you to know how it's all going. The method I used—and there are many others—was to keep a class list on a clipboard and twice a week to write observations for each child—just brief notes—what he worked on at project time, insights attained, problems encountered. I found a twice-a-week note was sufficient to give me a longitudinal view and also to help me be sure that I had indeed observed every child!

Then I kept a notebook for writing conferences—the child's subject matter, author skills, spelling, joy in writing, and another notebook for reading conferences! Kids can help keep track of their reading by keeping a list of what they read (we had a form for that, too) and turning in these lists when their page is full.

Portfolios are also good. They're concrete embodiments of what a child has done, good for sharing at family conferences and for you and the child to look at together now and then in order to jointly assess progress and plan next steps. What a nice idea, don't you think, for the child to be part of assessing his own work, for developing his criteria for what is good work and how to decide what to work on next?

Build the portfolios with the kids. Ask them maybe once a month to select a piece of writing they feel is either their typical or their best (this must be edited and nicely copied). You might want to include the first drafts to show the process. Include pieces of art—painting, weaving, sewing. Maybe take a photo of a piece of construction. In the writing, maybe one piece of fiction, one poem, one factual piece—whatever seems appropriate—and date each. I know the portfolios sound like a forbidding piece of work! They *are* a lot of work, but look at the time spent doing it as part of a teaching-learning piece. You and the child reviewing and thinking about his work; you with the opportunity to hear the inner workings of the child's process; the child self-evaluating and helping set standards for self-growth, self-responsibility. Isn't that incredibly important for learning throughout life?

Dottie

∞

Dear Sam,

You're still worrying about assessment. That's fine. At the beginning of the year, ask a more experienced colleague to show you an "about grade level" book and look at the city curriculum guide for an "about grade level" math. Know you'll have kids above and below. That may help you feel more comfortable.

But look at how much you've learned about your kids just in this last week of working with them! How would you assess the kids as they worked in your homeless unit? Who had lots of ideas, who took leadership roles in organizing the group work, who worked with energy over time. Who knew where to locate resources for research, who constructed something and demonstrated understanding of physical relationships and the properties of construction materials. Who was able to explain/present the group's work to the class. Who could read what for information. Who got discouraged as soon as something didn't work. Who needed lots of teacher support. These are the things that tell you about the kids as learners. Plus you know what they're up to in math, plus where they are in reading—from reading with them. That's it!

Dottie

∞

Dear Sam,

Thanks for the journal. I am so pleased with all you've learned and with your upbeat way of handling the learning that comes when things don't work as planned. A good attitude.

Re: the child and his family conference. After the discussion, was a plan drawn up with his help to show what he would change and how he planned to do it? Did the plan include where he felt his parents or teacher could help him? Such a plan should be short term and deal with a realistic number of situations—not a one hundred percent overnight change expected. Then you also set a time (two weeks hence, maybe) for another conference to discuss successes, modifications needed in the plan, etc. "I'll be good" is too vague. "Good" and "bad" are too broad as categories. That's why he gives the shrug of the shoulders. He really doesn't know how to handle it. A concrete plan is needed. Maybe even "When I start to feel angry, I will [action to take]."

I'm so excited by the way you are managing with Roger, that you know he always has to say "No" before he can say "Yes" and that you are able to allow him to say it. It doesn't become an issue of "My authority is threatened." Terrific!

Dottie

⌒

Dear Vera,

Like you, I found older kids harder to deal with than little ones. Maybe because my own adolescence was so painful that when I see kids dealing with theirs, it makes me scared and angry all over again. Unsolved personal issues in my case.

What you're seeing, I think, is preadolescence, that terrible time when kids begin to see themselves as adults—separate from us, independent, with their own ideas and values, and, at the same time, very scared about this new role—knowing that they're still not competent. Being unsure, being scared, they have to put on a show—be nasty, defiant. When a person is really comfortable with himself, he doesn't need to do these things!

The "Shut up" and other language does need to be dealt with—in nonpunitive ways—to build a sense of community. It should not, if possible, be tied to authority issues—you versus them, teacher versus student. It's too sensitive. And it's not what you want anyhow. You want it to be us—family, team.

Games can teach cooperation. But, like you, I'm skeptical about carryover. In a discussion, one could have kids think about how they do cooperate in a game—their methods, techniques for so doing, and then discuss whether/how these techniques could be used in a classroom to create the team. But don't lecture, don't preach. Let it be a serious discussion. And if there's no solution agreed to, so be it. Just let them know that the problem still needs to be solved, so the group will need to do some more thinking, studying of the issue, and solution seeking. Think how much education is going on—even without an immediate solution—identification of problems, issues, feelings, others' points of view, group responsibility, individual responsibility, verbalizing, discussing, and thinking—wonderful!

Dottie

∽

Dear Vera,

I, too, do not understand why many kids are late or absent. Kids are supposed to be on time. The teacher needs to find out why and needs to be in touch with parents. We don't know where the problem lies until we check. I once had a kid who left home on time but never got to school on time. Having his own adventure each morning. The parent was shocked, as we were, when we found out. Reprimanding won't tell us why it happens. Nor will it help us know what to do.

It may be that the parent and kid need to be helped to make a plan. Is there an alarm clock? Whose responsibility is it to see it's set? How much time needs to be allowed between alarm ring and leaving for school? Who gets breakfast? You may need a family conference to do this! Don't assume the parent is at fault. Your attitude will show and will be counterproductive! Be understanding, and be supportive.

When do we hold children responsible for themselves? As soon as they are able. Our job is to help them become able. To do that, we need to find out what the problem is. Avoid moral judgments. Think in terms of what concrete steps might be suggested to make getting to school on time an achievable goal.

Dottie

∽

Dear Vera,

Good for you that you didn't "butt heads" with the student and good you found her nastiness humorous. That shows you are realizing that she is a child and that you are an adult, and thus you don't respond child to child. And then she responded just as you would want her to—came to talk with you about the book! Like the three-year-old who says, "I hate you!" and two minutes later wants to sit on your lap!

Re: not giving a student a "smart" remark if they say something "smart." Do you like their "smart" remarks? Is that the way you want them to speak?

If you speak to them in the same sarcastic way, what message are you giving them? You write in your journal, "Dogs understand dogs, and cats understand cats," but neither you nor they are cats or dogs. You are human beings. I'd like you to write something more on this in your next journal and deal some more with issues of role models and what you see as "authority" and "respect." What are some of the ways respect might be earned, obtained, and "authority" be deserved and recognized?

Also, related to the above—what kind of learners and adults do you want your students to become? The "Yes, sir," "No, sir," and "I'll be good because there's a cop looking" kind, or the independent thinking, internally moral type? How might school experience affect the outcome? Please respond.

Re: teacher's role in a discussion. The teacher's role is to encourage children to express their ideas, to deepen the children's thinking about their own ideas, to consider (which is more than listen to) others' viewpoints and to do more research about these ideas where appropriate—all to help children understand more deeply and to think more objectively. The teacher does this by accepting all points of view (whether or not he agrees with them), by asking questions such as, "Could you explain that further? Have you had an experience like that?" This questioning encourages the child to explore more deeply his own point of view and its source. The teacher then asks other children for their ideas. "Have others of you had a similar experience? Who has another point of view? Tell us about that." If the discussion is not rich enough, the teacher may give some examples of situations he thinks children may have had which relate to the current situation and which might help them understand better. He may ask for some research. Even little kids can research—by interviewing their parents.

The teacher does it also by modeling a quiet, thoughtful, respectful, accepting tone of voice, so thinking can happen. It's not an issue of who will win but of setting a tone for considering ideas and for thinking things through. When children ask a teacher, "What do you think?" it's often important for a teacher to say, "What I think doesn't matter right now. It's what you think and how you arrive at your point of view that matters."

A teacher who jumps in with his own point of view is likely to cut off the kids' exploration, because the authority has spoken. The teacher must speak when authority needs to make itself felt, but that is not the point of a discussion. *The point of a discussion is to make clear the many-faceted*

Figure 5.1 Six-year-olds at the water table experiment with funnels, tubing, a turkey baster, and a water wheel.

aspects of almost everything and to promote thinking and understanding, not necessarily even to come to an agreement.

You write that you feel the program encourages you to give "too much responsibility" to children. You give as examples the child's choosing her own book, learning what she wants to learn, and you contrast "child" with "student." The child becomes a student apparently only when she learns what the teacher has planned—I think you mean has directed her to learn.

So let's look at that. We've spent a number of lunch meetings exploring possible learnings in a learner-centered classroom. Let's look at it again. Let's take a pre-K/K and a fifth/sixth grade.

In the pre-K/K, the teacher has set up cooking, water table, painting, construction, sand, and blocks. By so doing has he—as teacher—planned something for the children to learn? Of course he has. He has set up an environment where things will be learned. Will all the children learn exactly the same thing? Will they all learn it in the same order? At the same time? Does it matter?

Are there any advantages to having the children choose which of these activities they want to do? In the fifth/sixth grade room, you observed that some of the children chose to build a dollhouse. A neighbor and friend dissected a fish. Two others examined a collection of real bones. A small group made paper. Would it have been better if they all made houses, all dissected fish, or all did something that they didn't care about that the teacher had decided on? What might be the advantages/disadvantages of each method? Again, does choice make any difference in the learning, and what is its relationship, if any, to learning?

Incidentally, did you notice the number of children using books (not a single classroom science text, but different books) for information they needed for their project? We usually think of "project time" as hands-on work and exploration, but project-related research from books logically fits. Was the availability of books part of what the teacher planned?

Also, hazard a guess as to plans the teacher may have made in order that these different projects could take place simultaneously. Can you guess what teacher interventions he might have planned during the life of each project?

In your next journal please write down your ideas on cats and dogs and your responses to my questions on choice/teacher plans, and we'll go the next step.

I'm glad you raised these basic educational issues. Many thanks!

Dottie

∞

Dear Vera,

You raise a question about heterogeneous classrooms and the difficulty of meeting all the children's needs when some need so much attention.

You ask "How can one teacher handle so many children, especially when there's so wide a range in their skill levels?"

It takes a lot of thought and a lot of planning, and I'm not sure what the "optimum" teacher/student ratio would be. When I taught eight- and nine-year-olds, I thought twenty-five seemed ideal. If there are too few, you lose the wonderful interactions and fertilization that happens when a group is big enough and heterogeneous enough to have lots of styles, personalities, experiences, and ideas! The trick is to set up your classroom so that the materials and activities themselves teach and so that children learn to teach themselves and to teach and work with their peers.

It's true some kids need lots of attention. One of the joys of a heterogeneous multiage grouping like we have at CPE is that you can give it to

Figure 5.2 "You can make big, long bubbles, little or big. I made one shaped like a dog house. It gets more air when I blow it." This seven-year-old is focused on size. Later he may notice the "rainbow" of colors on the bubble's surface, the reflection (sometimes upside down) of ceiling fixtures. He may notice the change in shape, experiencing the effect of gravity and surface tension, experiencing the surface-area-to-volume relationship.

them! Some of the kids will need very little attention. You'll have them tell you what they want to study. You'll discuss their questions with them. You'll help them make a plan about how to find out what they want to know, and off they go! You'll only need to check with them now and then. Others you'll pair up (actually, they'll do it themselves), so they can help each other. They, too, will need you only minimally. And you're free to help those that mainly need you—or mainly need you for some things.

Think how much more children will learn in your classroom because you help them discover how little they need you, how well they can learn on their own or by working with peers. It will be a great classroom with you giving to each—not the same amount of attention—but to each according to his need.

Dottie

∞

Dear Vera,

I agree with you that it's important that all kids work in school. To know how to maximize the work, you have not only to set up the classroom routines and environment to support it (helping kids make good choices, having resources available, ways to keep track, ways for kids to report progress, etc.), but you have to know each kid as an individual. Because there may be different reasons why different kids don't work. And, I'm sure you know that no matter what you do, all kids will not work equally hard or well or equally hard at the same things. So perhaps note which kids goof off a lot and see if you can find a pattern, a reason, and then think how you might work with that kid.

Parents and teachers. There has long been distrust between teachers and parents, each blaming the other for what the child can't do! CPE looks at parents as real and valuable partners. It's not merely a "See that your child does the homework I send home" sort of relationship. It's a "Tell me about your child so I can understand him better; share your knowledge with me, so I can do a better job with him" relationship. When teachers reach out this way to parents and a friendly, trustful, and respectful relationship is established, things work ever so much better.

I'm so pleased with how much you've observed and thought about. I'm looking forward to the next journal installment.

Dottie

∞

Dear Vera,

Thanks for the next installment.

Re: writing and grammar. It's true that as children read they will "hear" the Standard English and many will adopt it for their writing without its having to be taught. But not all kids will. If we ignore punctuation errors and nonstandard spelling and grammar, the danger is that the message we send is that those things don't matter—when they do!

So I think the idea is to put each aspect of writing in a sensible place. First drafts, second drafts should be for creativity and effectiveness of the writing. Final drafts—before publishing—should be for the mechanics.

That's one of the things that's so useful about your class newspaper. It publishes often enough that it provides practice in these mechanics in a very sensible framework.

There are several ways to handle mechanics. You might partner kids up to check each other's work as a starter before you do final check. You might try the minicourse method for groups of kids needing the same kind of help. You can also have kids who serve as spelling helpers—those whose own spelling is good. Just don't overload them with helping others so they don't get to write themselves! In a class of eight- and nine-year-olds I usually had six or eight whose spelling was so nearly perfect they could be "official" helpers. The list got longer as the year went on.

For kids who worry so much about spelling that they can't write, there are several techniques. First, try really hard to get them to use nonstandard spelling. If they worry about spelling, they'll never get an idea down on paper. You can also say, "Write a half page, then wave at me, and I'll come help with your spelling," or ask the kid what words he thinks he'll need and write these on scrap paper for him.

Dottie

∞

CHAPTER 6

White Teacher in the Classroom ∞ Values in the Classroom ∞ Setting Expectations for Work

∞

This class is extremely diverse. It is interesting to be in a place in which I am the minority. The majority of students are Hispanic or Afro-Americans. Students use different words to describe feelings. They listen to different music. They dance differently. It's interesting, but a little unnerving because I am hoping I can connect with each one of them. I hope I can figure out their culture, what's important to them, how they speak to each other, what they talk about, how they see themselves, what their lives are like outside of school. This is stuff I took for granted before . . .

Beth

These fifth/sixth graders are very rebellious in that they are really asserting their independence. You can't help but love it and rue it all at once! . . .

Beth

I realized today that I overlooked that they are still children. They act tough, but they are still prone to tears . . . "Who am I, who do I want to be, how do people see me?" overloads their systems . . .

Beth

It's hard being a minority. I don't understand some or most of their feelings, behavior, conversations. I feel like a foreigner. I don't know how to talk to them. I value certain things. How do I impart knowledge and learning in the context of what they value? I don't know what they value. What if I don't value it? Students are subject to their teachers' values. I never have been one to say that my values are "right." Is it fair to impart my values to students? In a way, I'm going to have to say, "These values are the ones. They're the right ones." I'd like to think that there are values or maybe ideals that transcend cultural boundaries. Supposing I come up with a few, the problem then becomes how to communicate them . . . I think my main job is to help students be critical thinkers and to develop the skills to improve the quality of their lives . . .

Beth

- White teacher in a black/Hispanic/working-class school
- Values in the classroom
- Setting expectations for work
- Teaching how to work in a group
- Learning as "fun"
- Learning as meaningful activity
- Dignifying work by insisting on quality
- Figuring out why kids don't work
- Helping kids learn group self-management
- Child-centered curriculums and magic results

Dear Beth,

You write that you feel uneasy being a white middle-class person teaching in a school that is predominantly black and Hispanic and working-class. Understandable. In a society that is so laced with race, class, and gender issues, the new experience of being out of your "own" familiar group can be anxiety producing—but a good learning experience for you! Yes? Some insight into what the "others" may feel when in "your" group.

You'll find the bridges. Keep listening to the kids. Tune in to their feelings just as you would with any group of kids. Say you don't understand, if you don't. Ask them to explain. I think you will find that most, if not all, important values are shared between you and them. All kids need to feel valued, as do all adults! So you will honestly value them, and, as they get to see you as the helping adult you are, they will value you.

You raise other, important, questions about values and whether a classroom has a "right" to teach values or whether it should be value-neutral.

I think it's okay to believe that a few values are better than others. If a classroom is to function, what values must be lived in it? *Respect for each other, for each other's ideas, feelings, needs.* Wouldn't you agree? Without respect shown for each other, without an atmosphere that accepts every child, how can every child learn? How could children learn to help each other? Without respect—and its corollary, support—how could we build that sense of a safe and loving community which makes the maximization of learning possible? So even apart from any ethical consideration, living respectfully is crucial to a good classroom.

Negotiation of differences is another value that is crucial. In a classroom, conflicts have to be solved, not by fighting and name calling, but by negotiation. We have to help kids learn how. They don't get very good ideas about peaceful conflict resolution from the world around them! The adult world is pretty bad! But we can't run a classroom where conflict is resolved other than by peaceful methods. We just need to accept that teaching kids how to resolve conflicts peacefully is part of the academic day and worth a chunk of it. Not wasted time taken away from reading and writing. And think of it. If we can teach kids how, then they can decide if these methods are desirable/possible in the outside world, and maybe we'll get better adults out of it!

Critical thinking. Definitely. I think the development of critical thinking is the job of the teacher. To raise the questions, to suggest the possibility of different points of view which might be considered, to ask kids, "What's the evidence for your statement?" "How do you decide what's a 'fact'?" examination of the issues—not the teacher's role to decide the answers—only to help kids explore the issues.

Passionate involvement in learning. Passion, the excitement of finding out, discovery—this is the motivation for lifelong learning. What we teach children when they're in elementary school, at least, is secondary, in my opinion, to how we teach. The how—our own excitement for learning something new or revisiting old learnings—communicates itself to kids. Our willingness, our encouragement of kids to explore their own questions tells kids that their ideas have value and encourages a learning passion in them. We only need to introduce them to the many, many possibilities for passionate attachment in the world we're learning about. If the passion is there, they'll go on with the learning long after they've left us.

So—there are four values I think are vital to a classroom: respect for each child, negotiation of differences, encouragement of critical thinking, and passion for learning. How, then, do you communicate values? By modeling them, and by setting up the classroom so everyone can live them, too.

Dottie

∞

Dear Beth,

It sounds like your classroom is functioning very well. I'm glad that you continue to think about and be concerned with value issues.

The idea of bringing societal social issues to kids through their doing community service is a good one, but you are right. It's probably for older kids. However, you can get at some of it with younger kids.

Study homelessness. Visit a shelter. Collect food and clothing.

Study waste of natural resources. Set up a schoolwide collecting and recycling program.

Is there a park maintenance program? We used to be able to help the Conservancy people plant bulbs and rake leaves.

A discussion of lack of caring and helping in society? Yes, but also have "helping" as a value in your classroom. Set up a buddy system between the older kids' class and a little kids' class for help with reading or for putting on their skates at the skating rink.

You ask about setting classroom expectations for work and how to enforce them. Yes, indeed, you do need to set classroom expectations for quantity and quality of work. Know that everyone may not always be able to reach them. Yes, everyone should take part in whole-class meetings. There may be a child now and then who cannot handle the meeting. Help him to the extent possible (anticipate), sit him next to you, separate chatty friends. If necessary, excuse him—to sit where he can listen without bothering folks, or to do other work, if sitting and listening are too hard.

Fair? Yes, it's fair. The rule is everyone works to the top of his ability, whatever that ability is.

You ask, "Should everyone be required to read or comment at sharing time in writing workshop?" Some kids find it really hard to talk with a whole group and do better in a small group or with just a partner. Some kids are scared to take the plunge and may need you to call on them so they can discover that they can talk. You might experiment with different formats to see what works for whom, and what teacher interventions might be useful.

Re: math facts. You are right about how hard it can become if basic operations are not firm. That's why enough time needs to be given to work with manipulatives and other math experiences through cooking, measuring, scale work in construction, tabulating surveys in graphs—so that the concepts are understood. And then math facts do have to be memorized. You really can't be at the counting-on-your-fingers stage when trying to multiply two-digit by two-digit numbers.

How do teachers at CPE work through their differences? First of all, they start with agreement, a basic agreement on how to look at children and learning—an agreement with the ideas of Dewey, Piaget, Duckworth, Weber. After that, there's lots of ongoing discussion—informally and formally—and, often, not agreement but willingness to allow for individual differences—and a lot of loving support for each other so all feel safe. The same kind of supportive environment that they offer kids!

Dottie

☙

Dear Beth,

Thanks for all the plans. They look good. Lisa has also started literature discussion groups and might like to see your goals and activities.

Your ideas about learning as fun/not fun.

Learning should be exciting, not necessarily fun, at least as we define fun in our world—as a sinful escape from important work.

What we try to do is connect the child to learning, by encouraging his exploration of his own wonderful ideas, and by bringing in our own wonderful ideas with the enthusiasm we feel for them. We try to structure the learning experience in ways that are meaningful for the particular kids we have (and this is likely to be different for different kids in the same classroom). Insisting on good quality work—which requires skill development—is essential. It dignifies the work. After all, if putting out a class newspaper is worth doing, then it's worth the work of writing well, spelling the standard way, doing attractive layout, and meeting deadlines. All these skills and habits of work now have a visible purpose, not done solely because the teacher says I have to do it, but because it makes my project a quality piece of work, one worthy of the time and effort I gave it.

When kids don't work, we have to try to figure out why. And then deal with it. Some kids don't work because they think they can't do the job. That's usually it. So then think—how will you support their work efforts?

We also suffer from our instant gratification and sound-bite society! Our society does not encourage postponed gratification, contemplative activities, long-term satisfaction. So we have to set the more productive standards in school.

It's not an issue of work/leisure or fun/not fun. It is an issue of choosing important work to do and then dignifying it, increasing our satisfaction with it by insisting on quality. Kids really do respond to this approach.

This age can be such a pain. It's cool not to be enthusiastic. Don't buy it. A little hammer now and then maybe to break through this shell to the real kid underneath.

Dottie

∞

Dear Beth,

I want to apologize for not dealing more thoroughly when I saw you yesterday with all the good stuff you are doing in writing workshop. Because, you know, it is good work. The objectives are well thought out, the overall structure of the experience has been looked at, and you are thinking of modifications that might make it work better. The kids, despite their apparent inattention, did participate and then functioned on their own while you and I talked. That's the biggest tribute you could ask for—for what you are doing with them. This is the way good teaching happens. You set up something, and there's constant reflection on what's happening and what modifications might make it work better.

My critique was meant to help us think about behaviors that you might want to address and ways in which you might want to address them. I think your idea of having them discuss what behaviors might dignify and show respect for the work and help the author is a good one. You are right. Better to have them discuss it in terms of helping the work move forward than for you to impose your rules. Let me know what you try and how it works.

Your discussion with Win about the advantages/disadvantages of heterogeneous and homogeneous math groupings sounds like a worthwhile one. You may indeed want to use different methods at different times.

I found that math thinking skills—problem solving—the discussion of kids' strategies for arriving at solutions—worked very well in heterogeneous, even whole-class, groupings. Kids' ability to strategize didn't seem tied into whether they'd reached the skill of long division or three-digit by two-digit multiplication. And the more sharing of strategies there was, the better more kids became at it. I remember once for a couple of weeks running we did a math problem on the board, whole class, for 10 minutes each morning, listing all the different ways kids could think of to solve the problem. They got so good at combining and recombining numbers, at using addition, and subtraction to move above and below a number to find the result! It got to be a kind of competition against ourselves to see how many ways we could find to solve one problem. I think our best morning we hit seven ways! And this was all "mental" math—visualized in the head without paper and pencil. (For kids who can't visualize this way, let them draw, write, whatever. Most kids seem able to do it "mentally.")

Anyway, it worked well. A lot of math can be fit easily into the integrated curriculums.

Building models gets into all kinds of measurement—lengths, widths, heights, areas, perimeters, volume. Graphs lend themselves well to any kind of data collection.

Do surveys when appropriate. Cooking, of course, involves all kinds of measurement, and with the older kids (from third grade on) you can get them into doubling recipes, or halving them.

Sequential math: You need to understand two-digit place value before you can grasp three digits. It might need to be taught in relatively homogeneous groups. Try to think what a kid needs to know before she can handle the concept you plan to teach (don't forget to keep using manipulatives) and make a group accordingly to learn that particular concept. *A few more ideas about child-centered curricula and magic results. The idea is not that results are guaranteed, but that you stand the best chance of connecting kids and learning when curricula and the methods, the processes of learning, derive from children's interest and are appropriate to the ways children learn best, including the individual idiosyncratic ways of individual children.*

Dottie

∽

CHAPTER 7

Losing One's Way and Finding It Again: Redefining the Teacher's Role

∽

The worst part of this week was that for the first time in the last two years I was discouraged. I am questioning if I should teach at all. I feel like I am totally unprepared for teaching the way I want to teach, in the kind of environment I believe in. Somehow I have gone wrong in my expectations and my limit setting . . .

Beth

I envision my classroom looking a lot like this classroom. I clearly see the learnings. I see so clearly that students can pursue their interests under a student/teacher-planned theme. The class makes a good deal of sense with respect to what I feel about teaching and learning. Why was it so much easier for me to define my role in my other classroom, which was part of a different philosophy? . . .

Beth

∽ Losing one's way

∽ Recognizing the hard parts

∽ The two poles of teaching—kids' self-motivated action, teacher guidance

∽ Defining one's role—Teacher as facilitator, Teacher as conferrer

∽ A "web" as planning device

∽ Scientists' logs

∽ A classroom indoor pond

∽ Modelmaking to scale

∽ When kids fool around

Dear Beth,

It hurts me to read a journal that sounds so discouraged! I think you are
doing fine, and you are not a bust as a teacher. You must look at yourself as
we look at kids—at growth, not at perfection. Look at how much you've
learned and how much you've done!

You've been introduced to a kind of teaching that you like. The fact that
you've seen it will help you keep focused on the goal as you teach and
struggle and stumble in learning how to do it. You'll know because you've
seen it—that it can be done!

The fact that you know what you want is so good! And that you want
the right things for kids is marvelous. You want enthusiastic kids, kids able
to choose, to think about what they want to learn, to "own" their work
because they've invested themselves in it, to work with other kids, or
alone—and all the other things you've written about. You are so far ahead
of so many!

Second, you've gotten experience in some of the very hard issues that are
developmentally attached to this fifth/sixth-grade age, and that make them
so hard to deal with. That you don't always get them to work as you want
them to is no failure on your part. Think of their agony. They knew who
they were when they were littler. Now they're changing, and they don't
know who they are! They're constantly experimenting, trying to find out!
Testing, testing, testing!

So the teacher's job is harder. Allowing, encouraging, supporting the
adult-trying-out part of them, a new kind of "respecting" in your relationship with them, and still your providing the safety kids need in knowing
there is an adult who will set limits, protecting them from themselves and
their own excesses.

It's also hard because the hormonal changes tend to focus their energies on
nonintellectual pursuits, and we teachers want intellectual growth so badly!

You've also learned a lot about teaching techniques. Your math lesson
that I watched this week went well. You were able to see the differing needs
even within that small group and to provide materials that would work for
each kid. You didn't try a one-size-fits-all lesson even within the group!
That ability to see what the differing needs were plus the ability to know
what materials and approach are needed is wonderful.

Look also at your writing group. They are now usually respectful of
each other—thanks to your intervention. They feel safe reading their writings to each other and accepting and giving critiques.

I've seen you working with kids on the newspaper—helping them figure out what they want to do and holding yourself to that "facilitator" role.

It takes three to five years to become a confident teacher. It's a real craft. It takes lots more talent, thought, and skill than anyone outside realizes! And it never gets totally comfortable because it's always a matter of reflecting and weighing and wondering if there's a better way than the way you tried.

You write, "I want kids to take responsibility for their own work and I want to set standards for the quality of that work. I want kids to be respectful on their own, yet I have to say, 'Sit in a chair and look at each other.'"

I do not think you have "gone wrong" in the area of expectations and limit setting. I think you are in that advanced stage of knowing there are two poles—the spontaneity, creativity, and self-moving of the kids and the limit-setting, firm guidance of the teacher—and you are trying to figure out how to bring them together harmoniously. There are teachers who don't even see there could be two poles. They only see the teacher-authority pole. They don't realize that they rob children of growth. You are far ahead.

Dottie

☙

Dear Beth,

"It's so hard," you write. The reason it is hard our way—at least when you're starting out—is because it takes time and reflection to discover the ways that work, to lose one's own ambivalence and uncertainty. The ambivalence and uncertainty are what the kids so often pick up on, and then we feel disrespected. It's especially hard if we have to shed, as most of us do, the kind of educational experience we ourselves had! We fall back into it without even thinking about it when we're unsure and only catch ourselves later. And then we feel ashamed! How could we? How could we not!

In many ways, you are pioneering (for yourself), and that is never comfortable because you don't know what will happen.

Defining one's role is the issue, and that doesn't mean defining it in general. You've already done that. You want to be a facilitator of learning. It's defining your role in each situation—when to let the kids experiment, including in how they deal with each other, and when to be the authority and set the limits.

The general way to proceed is (1) decide what it is you think kids need to learn (how to make good choices for what to study, how to work in a group or alone, etc.), and then (2) decide how to make those things happen.

When I saw your writing group the first time, neither of us liked their behaviors, and you said you thought you'd discuss with them what the rules ought to be in order to make the writing group productive. Good idea. Your goal: useful behaviors; the methods that might work— such as a kid discussion about how to get the group to function productively. It was a good idea. It helped them think about how groups work. Next they need to try out their ideas and then maybe with your help evaluate whether their ideas did work or whether the rules they made need changing.

And Win is right. Sometimes it's not practical to take the time to do it, and you simply have to shortcut it and say, "Get a chair and make a circle." In general, however, we want to do it the first way!

And in the final analysis you, the teacher, are the one who has to decide.

Child-centeredness means focusing on the children, who they are as individuals, providing for their individual and different levels of learning, their paths to learning, and interests. You give them the opportunity to experiment, to try out and fail at taking responsibility, but you are still there to judge what is working, what is not, what may happen and what may not. Look how well you have done this. You are so far ahead!

With love,

Dottie

∞

Dear Beth,

A good, full journal.

Being a "conferrer" is the best teacher role because you are focused on what that particular child is showing/telling you, and you are tailoring your responses (teaching) to those needs you see. And you are right, that your notes after the conference then serve to record and assess and provide the basis for your next interventions. That is planning. "Here's what I see about this kid. Therefore, it's appropriate that I work on———. Here's how I plan to do it."

The more experienced you become, the less you have to write out plans for each kid, but you will still make the plans. And when a child puzzles you or doesn't progress the way you think she should, you might want to write out in detail what you know about her and what you might try. Look at Tracy's lesson plan for an individual kid.(See Appendix E.) They helped her think out what she wanted to do.

You want to know how to expand the work that began with the trip to the Meer and the finding of a turtle.

I usually planned integrated units pretty much by the same method. I started with a "web." I took a sheet of paper and in the middle I wrote the topic (in this case, "Harlem Meer"). I circled it and then I free-associated. Whatever came to mind I wrote down and connected it with little lines. I've drawn you one here. That got me to thinking about all the possibilities for study that might be done. Not that we would do all of them. Some might turn out not to be of interest. There might be time constraints. Some might be too hard. But the web gave me a good notion of what the possibilities might be. Next, I did the same thing with the kids. Work on a large sheet of paper with a Magic Marker™.

You might say, "On Monday we went to the Harlem Meer. What do you remember about the Meer? What did you find out? What questions do you have?" And then write down everything. You can tell the kids that you and they will set up committees in a couple of days, so they should think about what they'd like to work on.

The next step for me was to analyze the web, to see what might be a logical place to begin; what projects might flow from the expressed interests and questions; what trips, what resources we might need. Then I checked out my ideas to see if the projects and rough sequence provided for language arts (telling, writing, reading, discussing), for math, for science, for art, for drama, maybe for music. And most important, as I developed the schedule—how many projects could I handle at one time. I don't want to run around like a chicken. I do want to be able to circulate and spend enough time with each project to help the group do quality work. So some of the projects—most of them—need to be designed to require minimal direct instruction from you. You'll have resources on hand, you'll facilitate, but they'll do the work.

And then begin. Sometimes after kids signed up for what they wanted to study, I'd start two groups working, with the other kids still working on some previous piece of work. When those two groups could go on without me, I'd start another or maybe two more. All groups don't need to start on the same day.

Then as the unit progresses, I suggest you have a group or two each day or every couple of days report to the class on what they're doing and what they're finding out and have them take questions from the class. (You write down the questions for follow-up purposes.) Doing this means that the

Figure 7.1 "How did yo make the tunnel part?" a classmate asks this six-year-old, as she explains her model of the Park Avenue viaduct. Her explanation and fielding of questions build language competence. Her oral report teaches the class. Later, she will dictate or write a report to display with the model.

whole class is learning something from the group; the whole-class questions, in turn, provide more stuff for the group to investigate. Group and class feed each other. Ideas develop. Interest grows.

I've drawn my web for you. Try one. Yours will not be exactly the same as mine, of course. There will be things I never thought of! That's the fun of it. (For a web on the Meer, see Appendix G.)

Also, it doesn't have to be a whole-class curriculum (although a water study is so wonderful there's enough in it for a whole class).

Ask Win those very good questions you have. If the science logs the kids are keeping seem weak, the kids might indeed benefit from sharing their entries in a class discussion. I always liked sharing (it can be a few kids each day). The sharing helped the kids whose project was being reported on to think more deeply about what they'd done, what was important about it, how they got information, what new questions occurred as they worked. Then the class learned something, and their questions, in turn, fed the group.

I, too, had kids keep "scientists' logs" when I did a science curriculum. We first talked about what might be important to put in a log—the idea of keeping track of questions, method and results. Sometimes teachers give kids a list of questions to use as a guide. I prefer to develop with the kids the questions or formats (note the plural . . . formats may need to be different for different situations). When you develop the formats with the kids, the guides that result derive from their experiencing and make sense to them. In our scientists' logs, both words and illustrations (drawings) were acceptable. That makes it possible for everyone, regardless of writing skills, to do a log.

A wall chart where all children post their observations is an alternative that also works.

Glad you got in on some parent conferences. Ellie's "laziness" undoubtedly reflects her sense that she can't do. After all, why risk when chances are the result will be a failure? I know Win covered all possible bases. Can the older brother help with homework instead of mom? Is there an after-school program combining sports and help with homework? It would be great to replace the TV set with something more active!

Good idea to have Gina take notes for the group during writing workshop. Gives her something to do and keeps her in focus.

How to inspire better-quality writing? Ask Win. She's an expert, and I'm sure she can also suggest some books for you to read. Talking to kids about structure is unlikely to do it. Reading, sharing together examples of good writing will help them understand it, and you can also give writing assignments now and then to try out different structures. They'll moan and groan, but that's okay. You do want to keep ownership of the writing in their hands, but you also need to widen and deepen their experiences with doing the writing so they can improve.

More on the Meer. Can you create a mini-Meer in the classroom? One year another teacher and I used a child's wading pool and had the kids pour in the water, duckweed, leaves, muck, and creatures we had collected from one of the park's ponds.

It was great to watch the duckweed multiply. If I remember correctly, we had some tadpoles that grew into frogs that one by one disappeared. Too many crayfish! It does take a balance to keep a pond alive! We were sad to lose our frogs, but it was good science learning.

Dottie

Dear Martha,

Thanks for the perceptive journal and the good questions. You comment on the small amount of formal instruction that you see. Yes, in learner-centered classrooms there is generally relatively little formal, whole-class instruction. Most teaching is done as a facilitating intervention. For instance, the doll-house and mall construction. At third/fourth-grade levels, kids can handle model making to scale, and their models should be required to be to scale.

The teaching involves your saying, "If this cardboard person is the person who is going to use the house, how big do the rooms need to be? How wide should you make the doors? Can he see out the windows? Is the bed long enough to hold him?" These are questions designed to help the child think about what he needs to know and do for his project to succeed. You're not giving him answers. You are guiding his thinking so he will come up with his own answers, which will derive from his own examination of the world and its relationships.

I once asked a child, "Do you want the living room to be between the kitchen and the dining room?" The child said, "Yes, so the mother can keep an eye on the kids while she cooks." Not your standard architectural plan but a mighty good and thoughtful idea.

Your next teacher intervention with the child is to see if she knows how to do the measuring. "Which will you use—the 12-inch ruler or the yard-stick for this? How will you be sure your walls are the same height at each end?" And here you may need to do some direct teaching. The skill will be taught in the context of a real-life situation, when the child needs and wants the skill, thus maximizing the potential for learning and relating the purpose of the skill to real life. And, of course, if some other child already knows how to do this, you'll free yourself up to leave, having a peer teach.

You can see that all of this is math as well as language arts—as the child explains her project to the class, draws a plan of it that she labels or writes a report at completion.

How serious should this work be? Very serious. Kids' projects should be required to be as full a learning experience as the kids can handle. Kids who fool around are telling you something.

Check out these possibilities. (1) They made a bad choice of project. It didn't really interest them so they're not engaged, in which case you need to help them think out a better choice, something that they commit to for a number of days, at least, and will work seriously at. (2) Something else is more important—their behaviors, social interactions. This might be handled in several ways, depending on what you think causes a child to behave this way (worth a full discussion in its own right). (3) They need help learning how to plan their work. This calls for a conference with you. What are they doing? What will they do first, second, third? What materials will they need? How will they decide who in the group will do what part? Each child does need to have a piece to do, especially if you see a group doesn't handle this easily on its own. Sometimes you even need to plan with them how much they expect to get done during this hour and a half. And then the teacher role is to leave but to check back periodically to see how they are doing. There are times when you may have to come down heavy. "I see this group isn't getting much done. What's the problem? Perhaps you should work separately." And do enforce that, if necessary.

Hard to think out? Yes. Again it's the tension between wanting to encourage children to develop their own work skills and group work skills and, as teacher, enforcing the discipline from the outside—the limit setting! If you know what your goals are, it helps, but this is a matter of judgment, and we all make mistakes. Not a big deal, however. You can always change your mind!

One of the good ways to help keep kids working is to have a group or two share their work-in-progress with the class during meeting. It gives them pride in their work, makes that work important, and helps the incentive for getting work done.

A technique I used to help "teach" group work skills was to have occasional whole-class discussions in which groups reported on what was easy to solve in a group, what was hard, and how they resolved issues that came up. Different groups had different methods—as you might expect. The discussion gave the kids several strategies to use.

I remember once during a playground study kids were making models in groups and we had such a discussion.

I started it off by saying, "Today as I was walking around watching you work, I noticed that you didn't always agree with others in your group about how the playground should be built. I noticed, also, that different groups had different ways of solving the problem. It was so interesting that I'd like some of you to share your different ways."

One group of boys was very frank. They said they each put forth their ideas, but they usually did what one boy wanted. Another group of four said they'd given up on getting four people to agree, so they broke into subgroups of two, which was easier. A group of five said they'd argued long over what age group their playground should be for and then decided it could be for several age groups, with each member of the group working on the piece that interested him—a very sophisticated solution, I thought!

What time of day is best for projects? It doesn't matter. Whatever works for you and the kids. Some teachers do it after a quiet reading time; others after lunch. I used to do projects after morning meeting because I felt projects took a lot of energy—the academic learnings and the cooperative, social interaction skills. Energy is highest in the morning. Also I wanted to set up the work, check supplies, and so on and needed the time before the kids came in to do that. I usually did math after lunch, since that too involved getting out materials and setting up for different groups. I could do that during my lunch break, again before the kids came in. Reading and writing were usually a sitting-down, silent, or very quiet time, where chairs and desks helped maintain boundaries and energy for self-control was not needed. You can be flexible. You can change your mind. There's no one absolute right way.

Another thing to think about, however. Does the time you select for projects give a message of your feeling about their importance? Do we do the real work (reading/writing) first, when we have lots of energy, and save the play (as I've heard it called) choice time for the afternoon—if we have time for it? Or is project work so serious and important that we do it first off when our energy is at its best?

Dottie

☙

CHAPTER 8

Breakthrough in a Teacher's Thinking: Exploration at the Water Table

⬭

The boys were working at tubs of water using colored plasticene and trying to get boats to float by experimenting. They didn't seem to get the concept and kept making the same boats and only changing them just a little bit. I demonstrated one for them that floated. They could not explain why it floated and simply said, "I don't know." Then they began copying my model . . .

Martha

I watched the sinking and floating some more. It seems to me the kids are really just playing with the boats, designing different kinds, without picking up the idea why some are sinking and others are floating. Maybe it's something that with time they'll understand, even though the learning isn't readily apparent to an outside observer . . .

Martha

All of a sudden, I felt like I'd made a breakthrough and actually saw how an activity such as working with sinking and floating at a water table is supposed to work. I was so pleased with how involved and interested the children became with the issue of equivalency and how a lesson on equivalency came so naturally out of what they were doing . . .

Martha

⬭   Exploration at the water table

⬭   Hypotheses

    ⌒   Giving answers aborts learning

    ⌒   "Messing about"

    ⌒   Many questions can arise

    ⌒   Classroom management—meetings, transitions

    ⌒   Teachers as facilitators of finding out

    ⌒   A child who can't concentrate when reading alone

    ⌒   Math from playing store

    ⌒   More on boats

    ⌒   Oil and vinegar

Dear Martha,

You write that you were unsure of what to do with your "boat" group.

I think it will become clearer as you watch the children experiment with floating and loading their boats in the water tub. What do they say, what do they exclaim over, what questions do they seem to be trying to answer or explore? If you can't figure it out, you can ask. "I see that you are loading lots of cubes onto your boat. Are you trying to find out something in particular?"

Try to avoid demonstrating solutions. Lots and lots is already going on. It looked very exciting to me when I observed.

What is going on now is that the children are experimenting, making hypotheses (usually in their heads), testing the hypotheses, finding they don't work, and trying a new idea. That they jump from one thing to another doesn't matter right now. The ideas are flowing fast and furiously. You'll watch, take notes, and later help them sort out, go back, probe more systematically.

Right now they're learning about floating from the "doesn't float" perspective. "My boat had a hole in it. It sank. I try a paper boat. It sinks." The hypotheses—even if not put into words—are there, or at least a question to be explored is there. "Will paper float?" A hypothesis. "A hole makes things sink."

If you demonstrate what will float, you cut off all this additional learning about what won't float—the information as well as the raising of questions and the making of hypotheses and then the risk-taking of testing hypotheses. *If the teacher demonstrates "right answers," then children become afraid to risk trying things for fear that they will get "wrong answers."* Hold back. Time for "correcting" comes later—and differently.

In the process also the children are designing different kinds of boats. I saw houseboats, boats with flags. It's true that if they stray from the sink-float idea to the type-of-boat idea, they may not relate (or may not come away at this point with the ideas on sinking and floating that the teacher wants), but the straying opens possibilities for other learnings about water and boats.

What they're doing now is a stage called "messing about." "Messing about" may be a long stage. It leads to a "branched" type of learning, where a common beginning (water) is like the trunk of a tree and the different explorations are like its many branches. Different children may pick different branches, depending on where their interest takes them (their particular connection to the learning). Reread the two Hawkins articles.[10] They may be clearer to you now.

Anyway, so here we are. Kids are "just playing," as you say. What does the teacher do? She stands by (you can come and go between different projects, returning to observe as you can). She watches and listens and takes notes. She tries to see what questions or hypotheses the children are trying out. She may ask, "That looks interesting. Have you something in mind that you are trying to find out?" Or—to probe the thinking—"Mmmm. What are you noticing?" And don't correct misperceptions at this point! Make a note. You'll come back to it later. If it seems appropriate—that is, will not interrupt or distract the thinking, the teacher might probe, "Aha. And how will you find that out?"

Again: Don't give answers, but ask questions that might help the child to think. Later, after some more messing about, and before they get tired of it, you'll gather the kids for a group discussion of what they've discovered so far and what their hypotheses are, and their disagreements with each other, which we hope they will have.

At this point, you will help them see the various questions, and then focus them on designing ways to test more systematically one hypothesis at a time. "How might you find that out?" Now is the time for focused investigation, for recording of procedures and results (they'll see the need for it now), and later more discussions and maybe new questions.

Can you see the depth of this, and how you lose it if you demonstrate or provide answers? I remember once my terrible embarrassment when a visitor asked a child how he knew the thing he was explaining, and he said, "Dottie told me." Was the learning really his?

A classroom management issue to consider: You had a single group of four working. Fine, if you feel that's what you can comfortably manage. (And I notice you did just right in going over the "no splashing" and "what to do if we spill" rules and that you have placed a couple of sponges handy, since there will be some mess. Have dry newspaper available, too, instead of a mop, in case of major accidents—which seldom happen—but could.)

If you feel you can manage it, try to have several groups working. Usually two kids to a tub of water is a good way. The explorations last longer if several groups are working at it because you get a larger data pool, and they will look at what the others are doing and thus fertilize each other's thinking.

Incidentally, they are likely never to find the rule for sinking or floating (I had to look it up every time I did this unit, I found it such a hard idea to hold on to). What they will learn are the very many aspects of sinking and floating, and the learning will be deep and detailed and held onto! Think of this: Metal sinks. Can you make it float? Are there different ways to do it? Will a balloon always float? Can you make it sink? How does a fish stay under water? Do you float better in salt or fresh water? What about an ice cube floating? How can a bug "walk" on water? The building of boats leads to experience with volume and with balance. The loading of cargo leads to "fair test" issues: If I load my boat with just paper clips, can I say my boat holds more than yours if yours is full of washers, thumbtacks, and paper clips? A lot! A lot! A lot!

Dottie

⌒

Dear Martha,

You've raised some good classroom-management issues.

I, too, wonder why there isn't a formal transition from project time to reading. Projects are so active that I would think a slowing-down, quieting-down activity would be helpful. A quiet signal, like "Lights off," should be given, along with a "5-minutes to finish up" announcement, so kids can begin to shift focus. A 10-minute clean-up should be plenty, plus time for writing in their logs if the teacher is using them. And then to reading.

I used to like to have a meeting between projects and reading. It served a double purpose—sharing an interesting thing from one or two projects (e.g., a report from the water group on what they're currently trying to find out and how they're going about it), and then a quiet move—a few children at a time to get their books and find a place to sit.

If it's too many meetings, in your opinion, you might consider omitting the meeting that happens first thing in the morning in favor of this sharing midmorning meeting. You can do this if projects are ongoing, taking more than one day. You can lay out the work before the kids come in. Stop them at the door for a brief moment while they tell you where they're working. (Of course, you have a list, too, of who is working on what). Then they go right to work and you hold only those who have to choose something to do and need help to do so.

Re: Yusef and his book. I agree that you handled it well. Children at this school are used to having their viewpoint considered. If you think of what his viewpoint was—"I had the book first and you said I could read it to you"—you can understand his stance, even if you don't agree with it. Considering his stance helps in finding a solution to the problem (not the kid). Sometimes it helps to verbalize your understanding and sympathy for the child's view, even if you can't accede to it. Maybe, in this case, a compromise: "Oh, I'm so sorry! You were at recorder, so we thought it would be okay for us to read the book. Since we're half way through, how about your joining us and when the three of us are done, you and I can read it over—just us two."

Don't argue with kids. (I'm talking about behavior—not ideas.) Being respectful of kids doesn't mean you have to listen to a lot of nonsense. Listen when appropriate. When it's not, say, "Good-bye, get to work." Maybe when they get the idea that arguing with you doesn't work, they'll do less of it. Maybe not!

Dottie

∞

Dear Martha,

You note the shocking amount of violence that the boys write about. I, too, found it very sad and disturbing. Gives us a measure of what society does to them and why guns become so acceptable later.

It's always a tug between allowing kids to write their TV-inspired material and helping them see that they could really write good stuff. One year when I was teaching, the boys all wrote about monsters and the girls about princesses, and it was so boring! So I said, "This week we are all going to write true stories—something from our own lives."

Much moaning and groaning. "My life is boring. Nothing interesting ever happens to me." And so we brainstormed. This is a good way to introduce biography in literature and to help kids see the richness of story in their own lives. Of course, if they're writing about violence they themselves experience, that's very different from the reruns of TV that they put on paper and turn in as "writing."

Re: the graphs that you did in small groups and that took all day, with you working seriatim with each group. I agree, this probably wasn't the best way to do it. Can you think of another way? One that would maximize your input in a short period of time, and one in which kids would be teaching kids to free you up? Would it have worked to do a whole-class intro—a discussion of what and how—and then to have small groups working simultaneously, kids helping each other, and you circulating as teacher-of-last-resort? We do find small-group teaching to be more effective usually than whole-class teaching, but a combination often works well, and it's really important, both as a goal and as a management technique, to encourage—to insist on—kids helping kids.

At this seven-, eight-, nine-year-old level, kids can really teach themselves and each other a lot. You do not need to be providing information or hovering over every step of the way. One needs to rethink the teacher role—away from the provider of information to the facilitator of finding out. If the kids don't need to depend on you for everything, they will be freer and better learners. Can you rethink the project? What were the things they needed to know? Were there resources—books, examples, each other—that could have substituted for you? Could kids create resources for each other? Such as "how-to" posters for other kids to refer to? In planning, do think out as much as possible what kind of help kids will need and what resources you can supply that will give it. That's the way you have to think to teach an individualized curriculum in a room of twenty-five or thirty kids. It can be done! And you'll love it when you hear that quiet hum and see them working virtually without you.

Dottie

Dear Martha,

Good journal! And such good news in it! Glad the reading to the class went well and also running the morning!

Interesting that these third/fourth graders liked Cindy-ella just as the first graders did. You noted how quiet they got—you were surprised—as soon as you began to read to them. Books are so wonderful! I do believe kids should be read to everyday—for many reasons. It introduces them to books they can't yet read themselves. You model good reading, with all its drama—changes in voice, tempo, etc. It's got to increase their love of books. I used to read as the last activity each day. It brought us all together before we went home—a kind of closure.

If kids are out of the habit of being read to daily, you may need to start with short books for a while before you go into chapter books. There are loads of good chapter books. I'm sure your lit teacher can suggest some starters, or I will if you need me to.

Re: the book on bodies. Given that some kids want no part of it, I would guess they're not ready for the information. Having animals in the classroom that mate and give birth and take care of their babies might be the best way to provide the information in a way that children don't feel threatened by it. It's a step removed from their own bodies, and so maybe easier to deal with. The book can be used for a smaller number of children, as Carolyn did.

Re: Tony's inability to concentrate when reading alone. Does failure to concentrate happen when he's paired with one other child? Reading partners are often useful. Does he focus if his book is a book on tape so he can listen to a voice while he reads the print? Could a small goal be set with him to read a certain number of pages by himself and then could he spend the rest of the reading time with a book on tape? Would he draw/write about what he read, as a way of maybe deepening his understanding of what he read? Are there any physical aids for concentrating, such as a desk set apart and the chair placed so that he faces a wall rather than the rest of the class where he'll interact with someone else's roving eye? Does the resource room have any suggestions? It's hard to know what to suggest without knowing the child, and you may have to experiment. Try planning it with his help—in terms of what he thinks might help him to concentrate for longer periods. Good luck.

Dottie

∞

Dear Martha,

The mall continues to be of high interest. Good. Now might be the time to do a minimath unit on money and making change. Don't try it while the kids are pretending store. My guess is they are more into the role-playing part of "store" and don't really care if they give the right change, but you might want to do it at math time.

Re: punishing kids who don't listen to you read story before lunch. I wouldn't punish. Yes, I would stop reading. You have a couple of options. You could say (quietly, of course), "I don't enjoy reading this way, so I'll stop, and we'll just sit quietly until lunch." or "Some of you seem to want to hear the story and some don't. Those of you who don't, I'll excuse you a few at a time. Find a desk away from your friends. Put your heads down, and close your eyes and your mouth while I read." Don't read until all the resters are resting.

Dottie

∞

Dear Martha,

Your journal sounds joyous. How nice!

I agree with you. The math lessons seem to be going very well.

And I like the way you've helped the kids reorganize their book-writing project. Now you have learned some of the techniques! The kind of replanning you helped them do is probably what they needed to have a teacher help them with at the beginning, before they started the work. Since picture drawing is the most fun part, it probably is a good idea to let them draw a few—maybe five—to help the story line reveal itself. But if the writing doesn't start soon thereafter, it may not get done at all! So a few pictures, and then some text, with each kid writing some of it, and then pictures again, and so on. Good thinking!

Sounds like the water work continues well. Two boys said the clay boats had to be wet to float, two said they had to be dry? Great! A good basis for a small group discussion. Imagine. Two teams of scientists do an experiment and come up with different results. Happens in real life, too, doesn't it? How could that happen? Do they have any ideas why? What could they do to resolve the issue? A basis for further experimentation. It's exactly this kind of thing that you hope will happen. The final answer, you know, is somewhat less important than the explorations to try to find those answers, yes?

The oil and vinegar nonmixing: How did you probe that? Specifically, did the kids raise any questions? What did you ask them? Maybe nothing would have worked. You can't always know what will spark excitement and curiosity.

I once had a group that got interested in trying to make water and oil mix. One of the kids' older sister had something about it in a book. So I got them some oil and a jar and they did everything they could think of to make a mix. They shook and shook. They turned the jar upside-down. They stirred it. They couldn't believe it. I suggested they share their experience with the whole class, so at the sharing meeting they told what they had tried and what happened.

These are the questions the class asked them that I wrote down: "Which did you pour first, the oil or the water? Did you put in the same amount of each, or more of one than the other? Did you try pouring both at the same time? Was the water warm or cold? Would this happen if you used a different kind of oil?"

The next day I brought in some transmission oil. The girls tried all the experiments suggested by the class and again reported. Again, more questions came. It expanded to oil and vinegar, to water and vinegar. It led to using food coloring so we could tell which was the water and which the vinegar. It led to the need to label the different containers, to accurate measurement, to record keeping. Several different oils were tried; oils were put together. Throughout, the group reported to the class, the class fed the group with more questions and suggestions, and the group in turn fed the class. It went on for over a week. Even without an "answer" or an advanced explanation, look how much was learned about scientific process, including making hypotheses, testing them, and asking new questions that arise from the experience.

Re: the drawing. Yes, you do have a right to regulate their classroom freedom. The basic issue is, "Will anything be learned from the activity?" If the answer is "Yes," it's okay. If it's "No," it's not. *Children have the choice between options for work. They do not have the option not to work.*

Sounds like the trip to the beach to look at the sea was a good choice for a water study. What comments did the kids make? What questions did they ask? What "wrong" hypotheses did they make? A trip usually does not stand alone but is integrated into the classroom work. The logical next step is a classroom discussion. This discussion usually should not be an end in itself. The essence of good teaching is to build on what children know and think; the discussion should propel the work forward. What new interests were opened? What questions need to be explored? Make a plan.

Dottie

∞

CHAPTER 9

The Child as Central to Teaching and Discipline ∽ More on Curriculum and Management

∽

I think that one of the most challenging aspects of teaching is recognizing each child's strengths and needs and being flexible enough to have the lessons draw on those strengths and meet those needs . . .

Martha

So now I have a new goal: Don't worry so much about losing control! There is less of a chance of chaos breaking out if the kids are totally involved in what they are doing . . .

Martha

Simon fled from the gym. I found him crying by himself outside the office. I asked him to come with me. He refused. A former teacher came by. But he wouldn't talk to her. She told me it would be best to leave him alone for a few minutes. He usually requires some time alone before he is willing to talk. Simon disobeyed instructions at least three times. My question is, "Is a child who misbehaves entitled to time alone?" . . .

Rebecca

∽ A technique for teaching notetaking

∽ Dealing with Simon—removing defiance/authority issues

∽ Self-discipline acquired when a child feels safe

∽ Acknowledging feelings

∽ Choice important for meaningful learning

∽ Preplanning a unit

∽ Committee work

∽ Let the kids measure

∽ The value of a quiet room

∽ Taking away recess

∽ When a class doesn't function well, check curriculum, organization

∽ "I will not fight" is not a plan

∽ Positive feedback

∽ Inquiry learning

∽ Open-ended questions

∽ Inquiry follows inquiry

∽ When is enough enough

∽ Closure

Dear Martha,

You are such a joy to me! But you know that already! I love the way you observe the kids at work, critique what you see in terms of learning/ non-learning, what they reveal about the individual children's styles, interests and needs, thinking of other ways to teach/facilitate that might work better. That's how good teaching gets better and better.

I'm glad you looked at Tony some more. He may need lots and lots of support. Did you try any of the things I suggested in earlier journals? Did any of them work? You might try having him sit next to you during reading time and instead of circulating yourself to read with kids, have the kids come to you. This can happen very quietly. When you finish with one kid, ask that kid to walk very quietly to the next kid you want, and tell him you want him. That way Tony has the support of your presence, even when you are not reading with him.

When you start the reading time, see that the kids are settled in and reading, then take Tony by the hand and pick the book. Narrow his choices, since making a decision seems hard for him—maybe "This one or this one?" Then call your first reading conference, and bring Tony and the conferee to your table. I don't know if that will work, either.

Another possibility occurs to me. You might allow him 15 minutes to read with a friend (at your table), and then separate him and his friend to read alone "so you can discover how well you can read all alone." What's to lose? Try it!

Dottie

∞

Dear Martha,

Excellent lesson plans! As you always do, you used your observations to help you plan your next steps and to think about how things might be done differently for those spots that didn't work too well. You didn't just pull the ideas from outside the kids. You had these particular kids in mind when you planned.

You noticed that kids were copying verbatim from the information books, so you revised your plans to include how to take notes. Exactly right! You took your cue from the kids.

Have you a technique in mind? I used to tell kids to read a paragraph, then look up at the ceiling and think, "What's the one most important thing I learned from that paragraph?" Then say it sort of out loud, as if telling it to a friend, and write it down just that way. After all, what's the point of writing down the whole thing when it's already written in the book? Better to write it short enough that you can remember it and so it will be easier for someone else to read than the whole book might be.

I'm glad you saw how powerful the sharing of writing can be. Some writing we do for ourselves, like diaries. But a lot of writing is meant as communication with others. It needs an audience. Imagine a play without an audience, or a concert. It couldn't happen. That's why writers' workshop is such a good format. The sharing, plus the feedback for the author. Both spur the child to write more, and hopefully better.

Dottie

∞

Dear Rebecca,

Good journal! I like the way you talked yourself through all the issues and possible ways of dealing with Simon. That's exactly the way to do it! When you write down the issues and the possible ways of dealing, you objectify the situation. This way you can critically examine the alternatives, removing the "him-or-me" defiance/authority issues that so often cloud our ability to deal effectively with things.

Should a child who refuses to follow instructions "be entitled" to have time alone? you ask. Then you do your good thinking about alternatives and write that he may cope better when given time alone. I think you came to your own answer. What we're after in this school is not discipline imposed from the outside—the policeman, the punishment—but discipline acquired from within: "I'm moral because I believe morality is good." Self-discipline is acquired when a child feels safe—when he feels loved and secure with his significant adults, comfortable with his own feelings, and has learned acceptable ways of dealing with conflict.

So how to do all that? First of all, let's look at punishment. What does it do? You could take away recess. Call his mother. Scream at him with that big loud "You better listen to me" voice that we've all heard adults use with kids. What does that do? I think it creates more anger, more resentment, more sullenness, feelings already abundant in angry children.

If the adult (you, in this case) could say, "I see you're pretty upset and need some time alone. That's okay. When you're ready, you can tell me about it, if you want to," then you've given the message that you under-stand and accept his feelings (not his behavior), and you build trust and security.

You're undoubtedly right that his crying embarrasses him and makes him even harder to reach. You might try a gentle pat and say, "It's okay to cry. Even grown-ups do it now and then." Do that matter of factly; other-wise, he'll think you're treating him like a baby.

As for cursing out the gym teacher, I would think that's an indication that he's not ready to go back to the gym. I think I might have said, "Heh, you sound pretty angry still. Do you think you'd better wait a bit longer?" That way you are again recognizing, not condemning, his feelings, and you are asking him to assess his own readiness to return to the gym, where he has to control himself.

After all this is over, then the issue of hitting still needs to be dealt with, and it's only after all this that it can be!

When all is calm, then both boys need to meet with you together and use conflict resolution so that the verbal and social skills can develop that make peace possible. *And by the way, saying "I'm sorry" is not appropriate unless the kid really is. The most important piece is looking at the feelings that were triggered and the identification of better ways of dealing between people another time.*

Getting silence sooner after you flick the light: Some kids really have a hard time stopping when they're engaged in their work. We want that engagement. You might try recognizing that feeling, "I know it's hard to stop when you're right in the middle of something, but we do have to move on. You'll work on it again tomorrow."

And you can also be somewhat flexible if you feel comfortable about it. If it's a really big issue for some kids, and you're willing to be in the room during lunch, you might want to offer that opportunity to work instead of recess. Lots of kids love it, believe it or not! The ones who don't stop because they want to chatter are another issue. Use positive reinforcement and active ignoring. "I like how quiet so-and-so is. I see so-and-so can really hear me. I see so-and-so is ready." Then pause. "Good. Now I can talk." And don't forget when project time is about to be over, do smooth the transition with lights off and a 5-minute-'til cleanup-warning.

Talking at quiet reading and your being the bad guy: You're the good guy! They need to read, and you are there to help them do it.

Try putting the responsibility on them. "Have you picked a good place to sit? Can you really read without talking to so-and-so? Are you sure? Okay."

Then if it goes on, walk quietly over (unless they can hear you when you use a quiet voice) and say, "Sit over there." "Oh, please, second chance!" You: "Yup. Tomorrow. You can try again tomorrow."

Dottie

∞

Dear Rebecca,

You note how enthusiastic and involved the children are when they can choose what they want to study. You have it exactly right. Choice is so important for meaningful learning. It motivates because it connects to the child's interests, questions, and learning style. You harness his energies for learning. And a lot of the skill work can be taught within these projects, in a way and at a time when children see the need for and want the skill—all that math of measurement and scale and graphing, the writing skill of note taking and reporting, and the research skills, which include using a variety of books. How nutty textbooks are. Don't we really want kids to use libraries and see that information can come from a variety of sources?

Let's look at the choice list with which this unit was started. Whose "relevant questions" were listed—teacher's or kids? Might a question that is relevant to one person not be relevant to another? Whose question should be investigated if we want to connect the study to the child? Does choice have a role here, too?

That doesn't mean that you as teacher can't say, after a kid has listed her questions, "Might you also want to know how many people lived in a longhouse at one time?"—or whatever. That way you are suggesting enlarging or deepening questions related to her questions. Her questions are still central.

You actually did this when you took the undecided kids aside and asked them, "What do you think might be interesting to find out about?" If they have no ideas, give them some books to thumb through, skimming, looking at pictures, until they decide.

I think you are right about Marcus. You can't accede to his constant insistence on help. Try establishing his independence in small doses. Say, "I'll help you start." Give him 5 minutes. Check your watch and say, "I'll be back in 10 minutes to see how far you've gotten." Then do check back, even if you have to interrupt your work with another child. Making the time interval concrete may give him a little security. Re: the spelling. How about, "Spell the best you can. We'll go over it together when I come back."

Most of the other issues you deal with are management issues.

Preplanning a unit is crucial. In advance, the teacher has to think about how many projects she can facilitate at one time; what materials will be needed; what books, charts, other resources will need to be on hand. Often eight- and nine-year-olds can't read a lot of text from information books but can learn a lot from the illustrations in them.

You might find it easier to have "committees"—one for Iroquois housing, one for food, one for beliefs, etc. You can make them up from the list of questions that were generated at the beginning. Then you can meet with groups of kids to discuss their ideas, their plans, and their need for resources as well as helping them plan the how-to aspects of their work. And they can help each other so they don't need to depend on you.

When you're starting a unit, you may not be able to handle all committees at once. So pick one or two. Have activities not necessarily related to the unit (painting, cooking, math, reading) that the kids can do without you. Next day, start a third committee, and so on. While you're working with kids, others are calling for help. It happens. And it doesn't help much to tell kids to be patient. How about, as part of preparation for project time, you go over the procedures with the class: "What can you do if you get stuck and I'm busy?" Answers: "Ask another kid for help, do some piece of the project you can do alone. Tell me you need help, and while you're waiting, read a book or do some writing." They need to know what to do while they're waiting.

I like committee work because it fosters cooperative work skills, gets kids to depend on each other instead of on the teacher. Through discussion new and useful ideas come up, and you get to sit with five or six kids instead of only one.

Dottie

&

Dear Rebecca,

Good idea to do the feet-inch lesson at that point. even though it wasn't in the planned curriculum! That was the point at which the kids needed the information. A few questions: Did you measure out the 6 feet on the wall, or did you help them do it? Remember that kids learn best by doing. Also if they try to measure while you watch, you'll find out more about what they don't know.

For example, had you given *them* the yardstick and said, "Let's measure six feet on the wall," you might have found out (1) whether they understood the continuous nature of measurement (no unmeasured spaces between the two yardsticks), and (2) you might have opened the possibility that they would have noticed the inches themselves, whether they were interested in noticing the number of inches in a yard, whether they said 36 times 2 is 72 inches, or if they added on, inch by agonizing inch, from the 36 on the first yardstick, "36, 37, 38, 39, etc." This information would have been useful for math lessons further along.

You did nicely with the picture of the man and his igloo building blocks. Yes, do word the relative size in terms of the man. "How many snow blocks equal his height? Are they narrower than he?" That will help kids visualize the real-life dimensions.

"Vandalism" is a heavy word to use for pulling erasers out of pencils. I wonder if it's an age issue. My eights and nines used to do it, too. How will you handle it?

Would a class discussion be a way to start? Why should we not waste paper? Why should we not pull out erasers from pencils? How could we avoid paper waste? Do we always need pencils with erasers, or should they be saved for special projects while we use eraserless ones for first drafts? A practical discussion rather than a "vandalism" issue?

The kids have given you excellent chances for "teaching." A chance for the kids to think about the consequences of actions and then the chance to devise possible solutions. Don't throw up your hands! Use this opportunity to teach (facilitate the learning, I mean!).

Incidentally, has anyone asked, "How do they get the lead inside a pencil?" A topic for investigation?

Dottie

꩜

Dear Rebecca,

I'm glad you did so well running the class when Loren was absent. Sounds like you had the morning meeting well figured out and that you ran it well. I, too, like dismissing one group at a time to get to work. That way you can see them start, ensure that they start quietly, thus setting the atmosphere for the next group.

The loom construction: Did you and the child measure off even amounts for where the nails would go? Decide the size of the interval needed? Good math!

Dottie

꩜

Dear Sam,

You, like the others, are worrying about discipline. Important. We'll be dealing with aspects of it all year. Beware of taking away recess! Is it punishment or consequence? That's the first question you have to answer to decide if it's appropriate. Other issues: (1) You need them to be out of your hair for some piece of the day. *You* need recess, too! (2) It's the jumpiest kids, the ones who need recess the most, who tend to get deprived of it, so it makes them worse. And I didn't find that it made them better the next day. What other consequences can you think of? Might there be different ones for different crimes? Also, are there ways to anticipate problems and set things up to make it easier for kids to do it right? We want, as much as possible, to modify the environment when we need to so that kids can handle it.

Dottie

꩜

Dear Sam,

Thanks for the journal. You sound like you're having a good time despite how hard this class is—and it is! So many children with so many emotional and social issues. Overwhelming! Every once in awhile, a teacher gets such a class. Even a superb teacher (and this class has one of the best) is unable to get things to run easily and smoothly. The task is daunting; it is not your failure.

I still think punishment doesn't work well when a class doesn't function the way I want it to. A good place to start thinking about why a class isn't functioning is to look at curriculum and the organization of the day.

Is the curriculum suited to this group? When I observed in your classroom during the bug activities, the kids looked really involved. I didn't see fights or nonworking. Maybe this curriculum is just right for them: maximum hands-on work in small groups rather than a lot of sitting down, paper-and-pencil stuff, whole-class activities—these may have to wait until later in the year. When the work is well matched to the kids' interests and skills, you will find they work really well most of the time. A lot of nonsense happens when the work is not suitable for the group— no matter what the official curriculum and skills books say! If they need to be reached a different way, that's the way you have to do it. And that's perfectly fine! Look how much learning is embedded in this curriculum. All that science, all that good observation, discussion, prediction, hypothesis formation, designing of experiments, record keeping, reporting, searching in books. A really high-level learning is going on. The "skills" may have to be worked at largely through the projects—like short writing in the science notebook. So after you look at the curriculum and decide whether it seems appropriate to the group, take a look at the way the day is organized.

Is the routine one that starts the day off quietly? Maybe they have to be stopped at the classroom door, reminded of the first and second things they need to do, and allowed in just a few at a time.

Is the order of the day clear, so kids can anticipate what will happen next?

Are the sitting-down, moving-around, active, and quiet activities spaced in ways that work, or do you need to move something? I liked projects first thing in the morning when energy was high, and quiet activities afterward, when energy got lower and sitting in a chair at a table served to help kids with their boundaries. But experiment.

This group seems to have a hard time with a whole-class activity, where they have to sit quietly, wait their turn, listen to others, etc. Can you reduce the number of meetings? Maybe lay out the projects before the kids come in, stop them at the door, see if they can tell you what they're working on, allow in those that know, hold those that don't. When the "knows" are at work, take the small group that doesn't know and discuss their choices with them. Have only one meeting—as a transition to quiet reading. Projects, clean-up, transition to meeting—a brief sharing, or announcements, dismiss a few at a time to get their books. Since noise and focus is an issue with this class, you have to take more time to move them in small groups, which tend to move more quietly. You really have to work at order. Too bad. But consider that you are helping them learn how to become quiet and calm. They need to learn it.

Kids can have lots of freedom, make choices, and do good work while being orderly and reasonably quiet. In fact, I believe, better work gets done, it's more focused, when the room is quiet. Noise is particularly hard for those kids whose self-control is not great to begin with—too distracting.

Once you have the class as a whole into a calmer mode, then you can deal more productively with those few (and you will discover they are a few!) who still can't hack it.

Repeat offenders take so much time and so much energy! Ask parents to come in for a family conference. Discuss the problem as you, child, and parents see it. Ask the child what kind of plan he can make that might work.

"I will not fight any more" is not a plan. A plan is, "What I will do when I think Jason is bothering me is . . . " Don't forget to write down the plan, have everyone sign it, and set a date for a follow-up conference. Hopefully, there'll be only three or four kids you need to do this for over the long haul.

The kids who have a lot of trouble need this conferencing and also need a lot of positive feedback from you all day long. "I noticed how quietly you sat in meeting today. Good for you." "I noticed how you moved away from Jason when he was getting upset. You didn't even argue with him. Good for you," etc.

I like your idea of taking photos of the kids at work on their bug projects. Can they write captions or paragraphs about the work that could become a book and make a class book?

Dottie

☙

Dear Lisa,

I agree with your comments on respect. Certainly the teachers modeling it that you see at CPE is the first necessary step, but it's not sufficient. In our disrespectful society, we need to teach kids the mechanisms, the very words to use to live the respectful life!

You are right about the need sometimes to limit choices, especially if kids haven't had much chance to make them. Make it "this or that" at first. Gradually increase the scope as children learn how to choose. It's a learning, growing process.

Don't be upset about your angry reaction to the kids. Teachers are human; it got to your button-pushing point. Also forget about reasoning with the kids at times like this. Just say, "Cut it!" "Why?" "Because I said so! Just stop!" These are children. They still need us as boundary setters when they clearly can't set the boundaries for themselves. You'll be less angry at them if you do assert your adult authority and don't worry about being nice all the time.

Dottie

∞

Dear Lisa,

The book-making group has gone much too long, in my opinion. Here again, I think these kids would have been helped by your helping them set time goals and work division, leaving them alone for short periods of time and returning to them only to check on how well they're doing.

After all, what are you teaching them by sitting so long with them? And by doing some of the work for them? Only that whatever snail pace they work at is okay. That they can't work without an adult. Not good lessons. Contrary to learner-centered education ideas.

It sounds like your literature group is going well and that you are doing it just right. Re: responses to a book. I think it's easy to overdo the "write about, draw about, role-play about" stuff. Now and then, if you think these activities will add to the literature experience, fine. But the discussions you describe seem in themselves an excellent literature response! You're talking with them, they're sharing with each other all the important parts of that book. So on to another book!

If you're studying a genre—autobiography, poetry—you might want to do a piece of writing as part of that curriculum. Or do illustrations if you are studying how books are illustrated. Kids write a story and illustrate it in one or more of the styles of illustration they've seen. In a culture study—as when my class studied the Netsilik Inuit (Jerome Bruner's MACOS materials)—we read the songs and stories and then wrote our own. Same with our study of the Iroquois Nation. It's part of living the culture.

But as a "Now we read a book, so let's do a something to go with it," why not just enjoy, discuss, and read some more?

I enjoyed your description of what happened with Roger. He didn't look at the book dummy and so he had to redo the page he was working on. A good learning experience for him. One he wouldn't have had had you been sitting with him. Often more learning happens when things don't go well than when they do!

Dottie

☒

Dear Lisa,

Your questions about curriculum—content or process—and the others. Good questions. Content and process go hand in hand. Process leads to content. If the teacher sets out interesting materials or creates a classroom in which questions can arise and interest be stimulated, the *process* of the child's asking questions and the teacher's support for the child's investigation of her own questions will lead to learning of *content*. That content, if again available as the base for further inquiry (process), can lead to more learning. Content presented by the teacher as lecturer is unlikely to result in a child's learning a lot more content. The child needs to act in order to learn.

Sara's discussion of respect sounds interesting. Note she accepted the kids' ideas and feelings and was honest about her point of view. It was not just an adult-to-child lecture. Does this method teach anything? What?

Re: writing, it sometimes works to have a kid tell it to you and then say, "Great. Write it down. Just like you told it to me!" They usually look so surprised—as if they can't believe it's so easy, that the written word can be just the spoken word put down. No mystery at all.

Isn't it exciting when a "slow learner" comes up with an original and brilliant description! There are different kinds of learning, aren't there? Shows what kids can do when the setting encourages their own inputs.

Kids picking books too hard for them. Happens. Often to hide their own embarrassment at not reading "well enough." I used to take a quick walk around the room at the start of reading time to see who was reading inappropriately. You have options: (1) "That's a pretty good book. Would you like to take it home and have someone read it to/with you? Let's go pick one for now that you can read all by yourself." (2) Pair the kid with someone who can help him read it. At the beginning of the year I also helped kids think how to select a book—the bigger type is usually an easier book. So is a book with lots of pictures.

Re: reading "friend" as "father," if the word makes sense in the context of the sentence, it's okay to let it go (e.g., substituting "home" for "house"). Kids are reading for meaning, which is what you want them to do. If, however, the kid substitutes "horse" for "house," you need to stop him and say, "Wait a minute. Did that make sense?" A child should not be required to read word perfect, but it does have to make sense. The words will fall in place over time, so long as reading makes sense.

Dottie

∞

Dear Lisa,

Sounds like you did the whole-class meeting very well! I wouldn't shout, even to end an activity. If you want a quiet, calm classroom, you have to be quiet and calm. You have to model it. Use a quiet signal—like lights off. Then you can say quietly (when they've stopped talking), "You have 5 minutes before cleaning-up time" or whatever else you want to tell them.

I think what you did with Frederic was fine. He did leave the table, even if not with grace. Perhaps his lack of grace was his way of saving face. Maybe we can allow this bit of behavior, even though we'd rather he didn't do it. The point is, you established a rule for working and you enforced it.

I agree with you that some role-playing might help the kids become more respectful. A talk may be a good start, but words alone are seldom enough. To change behavior, kids need the necessary experience of trying on other people's skins and finding the ways to handle relationships comfortably. It takes practice. The classroom should give it.

Dottie

∞

Figure 9.1 A first/second grader tries her marble chute.

Dear Lisa,

Thanks for the very full journal.

You ask about kids' leaving their work during project time to go observe others' activities. What would be the advantages of allowing it? Disadvantages? Might you make different decisions about it at different times? If so, what would be the bases on which you decide?

The question of "inquiry learning" and the activities you see: hopefully the activities themselves are inquiry.

Two children are rolling marbles over and over down ramps in the block area. Are they "just" enjoying the activity? What's behind the enjoying? If you say, "Tell me about what you're doing," they might say, "Trying to find out whose marble will go fastest." That's the first inquiry. The second

Figure 9.2

1.

Which marbles go faster, the small or the big marbles?

1. The small marbles go faster, because the fat ones have more air risistens because they are bigger and the small one just got through the air because they are so small.

2.

What makes any size marble go fast?

2. The reason why marbles go fast is because of the down hill because if they are on a flat serfes after a while it will stop rolling but on a down hill until it runs out of momentum. An obtuce angle works the best because the marble will keep rolling as long as its on the angle.

marble

marble → → → O stop

A. 6
To make a marble jump the marble has to get speed from the downhill, then in like the middle of the track you put another ramp facing the other direction and it will jump like this:

7
A. To make a marble jump through a hoop. We made our own ramps and a circle. And on the ramp there was a little tiny jump on the block.

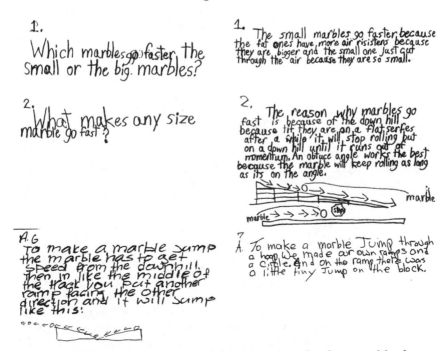

Figure 9.3 Fifth/sixth graders posed these questions for their marble chutes.

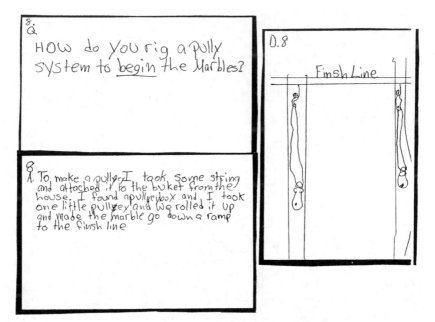

Q.
HOW do you rig a pully system to <u>begin</u> the Marbles?

D.8
Finsh Line

A. To make a pulley, I took some string and attached it to the buket from the house. I found a pulleybox and I took one little pulley and we rolled it up and made the marble go down a ramp to the finsh line

Figure 9.4 More questions about marble chutes.

Figure 9.5 Javier built a city around his plastic tubing marble chute. He wanted to create a chute in which a marble would travel around a bend with sufficient force to knock down blocks set up domino style. He experimented with the angle of chute incline and with the angle of the bend. The dominos didn't fall. He decided the marble needed to go faster and be bigger and the chute needed to start higher. A new construction will check his new ideas.

inquiry (or question, perhaps) is what can they do to make their marble go faster?

I'm assuming the kids are asking themselves some of these questions as they do the activity, even if they don't write them on a list or ask you. Watch a bit. See if you can figure out whether a question is being asked and what it might be. If you can't see it, ask the child, "I'm wondering what you're noticing as you work?" A very open-ended question. It may lead you into the child's thinking.

Extended inquiry follows this first inquiry and flows from it. You may guide it along, as needed, with your comments and questions and with added provisioning—like adding bigger marbles or "wondering" the question out loud yourself. The "unsure" part of it flows from a teacher's need to try to evaluate the experience. We don't always know what a child is getting out of an activity. We assume that if she returns to it again and again, it is meeting some need and is important to this child.

Then we still have to decide whether we want to honor this need for a longer period of time by allowing the child to continue it *at the same level*. But, don't rush it. We teachers always want "progress," tangible product results. It's hard to hold back and wait. Better to wait a little too long than to rush the experience and cut short the intellectual and emotional connection. As teacher you will, of course, try to raise or deepen the level of experience by asking open-ended questions and by additional provisioning so that more questions to investigate will arise and the child won't get stuck.

Sometimes the need to continue a project flows from the child's need to avoid risk taking and hard work he thinks he can't handle, which would be involved in extending his inquiry (Roberto's "I like it because it's easy").

Then the teacher needs to say, "Enough." And push a bit. The child either goes deeper or does something to bring closure and moves on to something else. (The teacher may want to provide support for the risk taking).

The next unresolved piece is whether the activity should deepen. Can the teacher think of important and interest-provoking extensions? If not, the project should end with closure. The child moves on.

Not everything turns out to have been a good choice, but nothing is ever totally a waste, either. Learning is messy and many branched, not linear. We don't always know where a path will lead. We as teachers have to constantly think about what is happening and how to guide it. There's not a fail-safe recipe that is the same every time for every child to be applied in the same way. And just as we ask kids to risk, we have to be willing to risk, too. There is no learning without some failure!

Dottie

∞

Dear Nicky,

I so enjoyed reading your journal. I particularly laughed at the kids' questions. "Are we done discussing this yet?" "Was that math?" Little kids are very open with their feelings and do give us cues about our work!

Re: Alma. You have picked up very important clues about her: (1) that she laughed at Joshua for having the same problem with spelling that she has, (2) that she was very upset when she was publicly reminded of what she can't do academically, (3) that she felt insecure about having to compete in math, and (4) that feeling insecure about her ability to do as well as others, she refused to work.

You have seen illustrated in one child many of the symptoms you'll see in other children whose learning comes harder and slower and who need support to build confidence. With such a child, you might want to call on her in a large group only if she volunteers. Perhaps help her start an activity. "Would you like me to help you start a pattern? Yes? Okay, here I go." Put black, red, black, then ask, "What shall I put next for my pattern?" and then gradually fade yourself out if she shows you she's getting the idea. You can come back after a bit and say, "What pattern shall we do next?" If she really can't do the first one, you'll know she's not ready. Find something else for her to do. Later in the year, as she grows, you'll try patterns again.

You are right about how good a circle is for whole-class activity. It takes a lot of space in a room, so when you set up your own classroom you'll want to think of how that space can be multiuse—that is, what activities can be set up there when whole-class activity is not going on. Maybe it's the library, maybe it's a space for math activities. Maybe several small groups could work within the space?

The worm and compost box project sounds great. The kids can bring in fruit and veggie scraps from home, and this time of year kids can pick up a few leaves and add them. You really will get new earth from it! Maybe you could even plant a few lettuce and radish seeds and then eat the veggies when they grow! Kids are experiencing the role of "decomposers" in the food chain, to give it the textbook term.

Dottie

∞

Dear Nicky,

You are working so hard and doing so well in unfamiliar territory! It is scary to do something so new where you are unsure of yourself! You're a good risk taker. And consider what insights into children's feelings you gain when you get a chance to examine your own in this risk-taking endeavor!

You write that you read an animal book to the kids so they could see how to write one themselves. I like to go back a step because I think it stimulates kids' thinking and gives them more ownership of their work. First of all, hopefully, there are some real animals in the classroom to study. If not, there should be—guinea pigs, a snake, fish, snails, earthworms. If for some reason this is impossible—though I can't imagine why it should be— you'll have to settle for pets, "animals I have known."

Then a discussion. Why might someone—or you—want to write a book about an animal? What are the reasons you might want to read one? Hopefully, this brings up the idea of wanting information. Next question: What are the facts about your animal you think might be important for people to know? Then you can show several factual books to confirm the children's ideas as well as to show the different content and different ways authors present their materials. It's important that kids see that not all books on a given animal will be the same!

And then, as they work on their books, you can introduce the various book parts like index, illustrations, and chapter and topic headings. But do start with open ways—the kids' own ideas, and the knowledge and acknowledgment that there are more ways than one. If you start with a model, you have already said, "This is the way. This is what I want." You give them a not-so-great message about what you think of their ability to figure stuff out or to have their own ideas—plus giving the wrong information—that there is only one way, or one best way, when there isn't.

You ask, "In developing curriculum how much do you, the teacher, need to know and how do you know when you've done enough? Plus, should you limit the share-meeting time to the curriculum?"

Good questions. Your meeting time should be used for whatever it is that you need to do with the whole class. If kids are immersed in the study and emotionally connected to it, they'll want to talk about it. Purpose of the share is to have small groups of kids sharing so as to teach the rest of the class and as a way to keep the work moving along. The kids who present will know they need to have some work ready, and the class may ask new questions for the group to explore.

How much does the teacher need to know beforehand? Enough to steer the kids into important learnings, but you don't need to be an expert. Learn along with the children. It's fun for both you and them, and think what a good role model you provide—an adult who doesn't know everything and is just as eager to find out as they are.

You might want to do a brainstorming session with yourself. The topic is New York City? Write down what you think you already know about New York City. What might you want to know? What might be important to know for a study in depth?— which is what all study ought to be. Don't just be a tourist. Be a historian, a city planner, a transportation expert, a sociologist, a geologist, a subway rider, a kid.

Your questions will help you look for some resources and get a little beginning knowledge, enough to start.

Dottie

☎

Dear Nicky,

Your journal is a pleasure to read, as always. You've learned so much over the semester, and you raise important considerations both for teaching and for the management that is related to it.

It is hard to move around and observe so many pairs of kids working. Remember, though, that you don't need to see each kid each time. Keep track on your checklist of whom you observed, and then you'll know who to look at the next time. Usually 3 or 4 minutes is enough time to spend with a pair—to ask them a question or two, to probe their thinking. In an hour's math (and you can do that much with second graders on up if they've got manipulatives and interesting work), you can see quite a few each time.

Your ideas for keeping track: good ones. Yes, make notes about who shares ideas readily at discussion time, who comes up with new questions to explore, who never talks at all (a teacher intervention needed?). Look at their drawings, writings, their skills at social interactions.

You ask, "Why and when do we ask kids to read aloud?" Good question! If you've seen those classrooms that have reading groups and kids read round-robin a couple of sentences each day, you've seen how little reading really gets done. The way to get into a book and read a lot of it usually is to read silently! And we want them to read a lot. So when to read aloud? (1) When we want to assess. You do that at the beginning of the year and then at wide intervals during the year. (2) When you're working with a particular child, one on one, where you want to intervene intensively—but you also send him to read with a partner or to follow a book on tape or to read silently whatever he can so he gets the habit. (3) Practicing for dramatic reading—choral reading for plays, poetry, practicing to read something to the class or to kids in a younger grade—in other words, when it's appropriate to the reading itself! And with very beginning readers, choral reading is a neat technique for getting them started.

You are observant to pick up the boredom of the reading group and to notice that they all wanted to read all of the story. Of course! Why not let them? The more print that goes before their eyes and brain, the better readers they'll be. I think the out-loud reading happens because teachers are sometimes afraid to let go and trust that reading really will happen—they think they need to know every day that a kid is reading—and also because, unlike you, they didn't question a time-honored practice, one that was part of their own growing up.

I saw in your week's summary that you had made progress with your "hard" kid by having him work with a partner and that he felt good about his success in the social sphere of partnering. Excellent.

In the case of Alfredo, I would suggest a friendly (and sincere) quiet chat about how you might help him sit quietly at meeting, and then lots of contact with him to praise improvement, to ask if he feels better about how he's doing and whether there are other things you/he might do to help.

Incidentally, I noticed that the teacher's eye catches him a lot when he's talking and that that eye does not catch the others who are! Watch out for getting tunnel vision about a kid! When you find that happening—and it happens to all of us—it's time to step back and think out how to change our relationship with him so we can see him differently.

Ask Tamara to tell you what she's done with Ramon. She gave such good tools for him to use, like asking him how he feels just before he gets so angry and blows up, trying to help him identify the triggering feeling. He told her he feels like he's sliding down from sadness to anger. She suggested he say, "Tamara, I'm sliding," when he needs help with self-control. Another day he said, "When you're not here, who can I say 'I'm sliding' to?" She asked him if he could make a picture in his mind of himself climbing back up the hill from the slide. He said he thought he could.

I write all this to illustrate an approach. It's not, "Do it or else." It's helping the kid develop the tools to do it himself.

Re: Velma and her writing. I don't know. Beginning writers often don't remember what they wrote. Was her spelling so nonstandard that she couldn't read it? If so, and if it's a usual pattern with her, you might want to "translate" it into standard English several times during the writing period. Maybe suggest she write a paragraph and then wave at you to come translate. You write the translation under her writing, and you read it together. A nice reading/writing activity. As for the spelling, encourage invented spelling as they write. Ideas flow better when children focus on their message rather than on their spelling. Most invented spelling turns standard as children read more and develop visual memory. Meanwhile, look at the sample you gave me. What can you tell from it about what the child does know?

Dottie

☯

CHAPTER 10

Teachable Moments ∞ Applying the Lens to a Sad and Angry Child

∞

I liked my reading group today because the students were engaged in a book they had written themselves . . .

Tamara

If the students' questions or comments lead us off on a tangent, I don't feel as pressured to get "back on track." I have begun to see that often the "tangents" that worried me so much before end up enriching my students' understanding in the long run . . .

Tamara

Ramon has a habit of hiding under a table, behind a chair, or in a closet when he does not want to participate. But he's making progress. He hasn't run out of the room for at least a week. Today he got frustrated that he couldn't spell "California," so he stomped to the other side of the room and put his head down on a desk. A few minutes later, he came back over to his notebook and said, "Okay, I'll try it." Then he proceeded to spell out the word . . .

Tamara

∞ Teachable moments

∞ Multilevel reading groups

∞ Learning that pleases the child propels her forward

∞ Anger and sadness

    ⅒   Finding entry points to the child

    ⅒   Helping the child call for help

    ⅒   Helping him to help himself

Dear Tamara,

This is indeed a superb first-grade room. You are right!

You notice how your teacher gets learning out of everything, including stopping her planned activity when the children suddenly noticed the pollen and flower on the plant and probing their "noticings" and ideas. That's called a "teachable moment"—the moment that children show you where their interest is, the moment that energy, motivation, is there for learning, the moment that you, the teacher, validate their interest by joining with it, helping them to observe more deeply, to raise hypotheses, and new questions. Those teachable moments are the best! A skilled teacher sets up his classroom in ways that foster questions from the children and so increases the number of teachable moments. (And, of course, you use teacher judgment whether to stop your activity at once or just briefly with a promise to make time for the investigation later—when in doubt go for the spontaneity.)

Isn't the "family" curriculum great, too! Working as your teacher does from the children's own families makes it so meaningful. Family is important to the child. And think how self-esteem issues and parental involvement happen without a separate issue being made of it. Each time a parent comes in to be interviewed by the children, think what message of importance and respect is sent! The father who came in last week wasn't a doctor or a scientist. He owns a bodega. And he knew so much and had so much to share with the kids!

You write that the hardest thing about your reading group was that the children were all on different levels. There are important reasons for having multilevel groups if you are going to do reading groups. One way to handle it is to do a lot of choral reading. You read first, the group reads together next. If any child is ready to try to read a page alone, that's fine. No pressure, no calling on kids who don't volunteer. Read the same story again next day. Kids love repetition at this age. They will especially love to read the same story over and over if it's been a group-written story, "their own," as you noticed! Little by little they will become able to remember and then to really read the sentences, and after that to pick out some words, and there's no reason why everyone in the group needs to reach the same level of reading of any book. When you and they have had enough of that story, go on to another.

It's great if you can find a book that leads you into a curriculum. Usually you can.

Almost any book about a child and his family and his pet could lead into autobiographies. Or just jump in without a book and tell a story about when you were a little girl—one thing you remember—and then group discussion and voila—autobiography.

You are so incredible with Ramon. He does need a lot of nurturing. Note the thumbsucking and finger twisting in the curl, a return to baby comfort. And so much anger and distress! A good idea that you suggested he draw or write about what he's feeling. When a kid can do that, it sometimes helps to objectify the problem and help him get rid of some of the feeling. A kind of therapy! If he can tell you his story, accept it. Be careful not to make judgments. And then, too, you may find his home situation has so overwhelmed him he can't deal with it right now.

Can you find some ways to help him validate his own worth here in this very safe and accepting classroom? He's so smart. Could he work with/help another child while he sits next to you? You're providing the adult support he needs, while at the same time freeing yourself to work with someone else and giving him a helping role as well.

If Ramon regresses in a group, can you sit him next to you, and, if necessary, put him just outside the group so he's out but not totally out? He clings to you because at this point he needs an adult he can trust. Security is a prerequisite to independence.

Can you help him with conflict-resolution skills? Six years old is not too young. Forbid the hitting and then see if he could think of something else to do if he's angry. Could he say, "I'm angry!" Could he stamp his foot? Could he tell the other person what it is he doesn't like and then come to you for help?

I suspect that, as you say, his anger overwhelms him. Maybe he needs help to recognize that and then help to notice in himself when he's about to get very angry. Is there some internal signal he could recognize? Does he get very hot? Very jumpy? Could he recognize such a signal and right away run to an adult for help —before he explodes? Let me know if you decide to try any of these ideas.

With love,

Dottie

Dear Tamara,

What an exciting journal! You can't believe how excited I was to read it!

It showed you're really understanding how to take your cues from the children and how to choose your teacher interventions to fit those cues; you are not tied to a teacher agenda rigidly prepared, rigidly pushed for in its execution. Your teaching is relaxed, child attuned, and therefore successful. Some of the teaching I've seen elsewhere seems so rigid to me, teacher directed for teacher goals, where the child's job is to figure out what answer the teacher wants, to please the teacher rather than to please himself! *The learning that pleases the child is the learning that goes in deeper* and propels the child forward on her own—like the *Chicken Soup* story you described. You read the story and since the classroom is built to provide for active child choices, this child for whom the story made a connection was impelled to find another chicken soup story—all on her own, all excited, without your having done anything more about it!

It's not that we don't have goals and objectives. We do. We know that if we create a classroom with stuff to do and books to read and time given for children to explore, among choices, pursuing their own questions, interests and ideas, we know learning will happen, and the "skills" can largely be taught within this context or in smaller spaces within the day. The intensity with which children work and learn in such an environment saves hours of teaching time!

Having said that, I need to deal with your question, "Why do little kids enjoy something as boring as handwriting practice?" Because it makes them feel grown-up and accomplished. And when most of classroom life is exciting and creative, kids welcome a little rest in the form of nonthinking handwriting. So it's fine.

Dottie

∞

Dear Tamara,

Good journal as always. I am so impressed with your work with Ramon. I think you are handling him just right and doing as much as you can for him, which is a great deal—love, support, opportunity to shine and enjoy, firmness-limits, and a chance to try to figure out what he feels and what he might do himself about it. I think it's astounding that you know when to do which of these!

Sadness and anger do go together. Sometimes sadness underlies anger, and suppressed anger can result in depression!

I think your working out with him the idea of saying, "Tamara, I'm sliding" is so good! It helps him focus on the start of the bad feeling, provides an acceptable way of expressing his feeling (saying it), and calling you for help. The idea of asking if he could picture himself climbing back up the hill when you aren't there to run to—what a superb thought! If he can keep doing this over time, he will feel much better about himself and you will have actually helped this six-year-old to deal with his life!

Your poetry group sounds great. A 3-minute discussion is just about the right length of time for the "How do we help each other?" discussion. Such short discussions are precisely what you need to do so children can work on their own.

Try the same 3-minute discussion technique for "What do I do when I finish my picture?" Kids do need to know what to do next, when they're working on their own. You might want a 3-minute share after the activity for kids to describe how they helped someone in their group. After a few days, try a switch: "What someone in my group did to help me." This is a brief switch from ego-centeredness to other-centeredness, from "What I did that was good" to "What someone else did that was good."

Dottie

∞

Everyone was busily at work. No one needed me. I wasn't teaching anything. It made me very uneasy . . .

                                                                                          Lisa

∞

Dear Lisa,

You note that one day no one needed your help and that made you feel superfluous and therefore uneasy.

Whenever you have a day when no one needs you, you will know that on that day you did everything right! You had the right amount of work set out, everything you planned was of interest to kids, matched their individual styles and abilities, and the work atmosphere was so absorbing that even individual animosities didn't surface. Wow!

On such a day you take your teacher notebook and you walk around listening, watching, recording/assessing. May you have many such days!

Dottie

&

Looking back on the semester, I think things began to become clear for me when I looked at the child and thought, "What might this child, at this age, be able to learn and how might he learn it?

Rebecca

&

Though I haven't really accepted all the new ways of teaching, I am slowly allowing myself to "let go" of my traditional classroom values and trying to step back and see the classroom from a different perspective. It's not easy to let go of the old familiar ways.

Nicky

&

The past two weeks have been remarkably different from my previous weeks as a student teacher. I have approached my lesson plans in a different way. Now I mainly aim to find subject matter that can grow naturally from the children's interests, rather than choosing some subject matter I would like them to learn and trying to find a way to force it into the classroom.

Tamara

&

Often my journal posed lists of questions for which I still feel I have no real answers, but they were generally questions to which there are no conclusive answers, questions with which I will be grappling for years to come.

Beth

&

CHAPTER 11

Getting Started

∽

As the end of each spring semester arrives, student teachers ask, "If I want to teach this way, how do I begin?

"Where do I find a school that will support, or at least allow, what I want to do? What if curriculum is prescribed, the order of the day immutable? How do I follow children's interests, provide for choice of work, and create the variety of entries into learning we've talked about?

"If children have not had freedom to choose, will they get out of hand? Who will support and help me as I try things new to me?"

To try to answer these questions, I interviewed four practicing teachers:

- A fifth/sixth grade teacher who began as a traditional teacher and moved gradually into learner-centered education (Alice Seletsky)

- A former student teacher, then finishing her second year of teaching at Central Park East 1 (Nicole Gadek)

- A former student teacher, with five years of public school teaching behind her, who pioneered learner-centered education in a traditional school (Kristine Annunziato)

- A teacher in a traditional school who, within a prescribed curriculum, provides some choices in what is learned and how children learn it, who has created a classroom that is a community, respectful of children, their needs, their ideas, their differences, one that builds their skills for independent thinking and learning (Karen Cathers)

ALICE SELETSKY (FIFTH/SIXTH GRADE)

B.A., NYU, in English literature and classics. M.A., City College, in reading. Thirty-three years of teaching experience: the first twelve in the South Bronx, the rest at Central Park East. Participant since the mid-1970s in the summer institutes at Prospect Center, worked on Prospect Archives of Children's Work, 1984. Worked with Ted Chittenden of

Educational Testing Services on collaborative research projects, including a major research study on how children come to reading (the first time classroom teachers were collaborative researchers with the "experts").

Be Aware of the School Culture

If you are going to a school for the first time, try to visit in advance. Ask to talk to the principal. Tell him or her you want to plan over the summer.

Ask who supervises, does staff development, mentors new teachers. If you can meet with any of these people, do so. Listen. Offer an idea or two of your own that could be used in either a progressive or traditional school. New teachers tend to be timid; don't be. Ask for guidance.

Ask about school reading, math, science, and other programs you will be expected to carry out. Get copies of the teacher guides. Read them.

Visit a few classrooms, if you can. Try to find out how well provisioned the school is.

Begin in a way that will not feel too challenging to what is already there. Not only the administration and faculty but even the children will need time to get used to new ways.

A former student teacher of mine said to her "traditional" kids, "It's time for lunch. Please line up." The kids sat bewildered, not moving. They couldn't do it. They needed to be told whether to make a boys' line and a girls' line, or whether to line up according to size order. The teacher needed to think out how to "teach" or explain the choice. What had seemed like a little deal was a big one.

Start the Day with Whatever the Children Are Used To

It's likely to be quiet reading. Start hands-on activities from the reading. Basal readers often suggest activities related to the reading. Do these—puppets, dioramas, drawings. Make mobiles of the characters in the story and hang them from light fixtures.

At first, have everyone do the same project—sketch on paper, copy on oak tag, cut out, etc. You circulate and praise for the social behaviors—sharing scissors, picking up fallen stuff. Explain the rules and procedures, including the sharing and helping, where to put work in progress, how to clean up, what do after they've cleaned up. Expect to explain more than once. Expect good days and not so good ones.

Other early projects: Collage is a good one. Little kids love shape books and writing and drawing books.

Kids should write every day. If they are used to being told what to write, start by offering one or two topic choices. Copying a poem works. Try a round-robin story. Start with minimal expectations for quality of writing. Once kids start writing, you can guide the improvement.

Math: If manipulatives have not been experienced, start with whole-class bingo. It's easy and familiar, and it's something everyone can do while you assess them. Introduce manipulatives slowly and teach how to use and care for each. Constantly praise for finding lost items, for good clean-up.

Increase Choices and Start Independent Work

When you have established order and routines, you can begin to increase choices.

Start with a subject area in which you are comfortable. If it's social studies rather than science, start with social studies. The curriculum may be set by the school, but you can work within that.

Think out what the social studies unit is supposed to teach and try to visualize how that information could be "discovered" (experienced) (translated) through art, drama, model making. The easier-to-manage projects are cut/paste, drawing, maps, and posters. Dioramas are somewhat harder, but terrific for learning.

If you decide to have committees to study the various pieces of the curriculum subject, you may want to select those committees at first yourself, to assure that there's good "social" leadership in each. Know that you will need to help the children figure out how to work in a committee.

Remember to provision in advance. If you are not experienced in working with materials, try your projects at home first. Get some craft books as a guide.

When you're ready for the class to try projects, think out what supplies you need, what containers to put supplies in, how you will have them distributed, and where they'll be put away.

Meetings

Meetings are secondary. If your school does meetings, do them. If not, you may want to wait until you have a feel for the kids and the class as a whole. Put the day's calendar on the board and read it with them.

When you start meetings, know what your purpose is. Keep meetings short. Praise children for their skill in listening to each other.

Parent Letter

The parent letter goes early. When you ask for supplies, be sure to say, "We need paper towel rolls, buttons, cloth scraps for projects related to our academic work," so parents don't think kids are going to play.

Nicole Gadek

> Kindergarten–first grade, Central Park East 1. M.A., Teachers College, Columbia University. Student teaching experience at CPE 1; two years of teaching experience.

My first year of teaching was hard. I had a classroom of twenty-three kindergartners and three first graders. Of the twenty-six children, eighteen were boys.

My advice is to get support. Find an experienced teacher to help you. Sometimes it's to take a few children out of your room. Sometimes it's to be your second set of eyes—to help you see what went wrong—to help you recognize what went right! In my case, Jane (the school director) was my eyes. So find a buddy or mentor to lean on. There was a gap between my teaching and my expectations. That's what created my anxiety. I felt like I was cheating the kids; they weren't learning anything. I didn't have any perspective. Teaching swallowed my life that first year.

You keep your vision by finding support from other teachers. It's okay to fall down. Get up and keep going.

Second, pick one thing to focus on. I picked community. In this classroom we needed to build community, so kids could feel safe, and we all—including me—could feel comfortable.

Kids needed to know what it was okay to do in each area of the room. We talked about that and practiced it day after day. Bites, kicks had to go. I tried to make it really personal for them, to help them see how words hurt or help. "Do you really know what you're saying when you say, 'You can't play with me. You're stupid. I hate you.'?"

There was this kid who answered for everyone, never gave another child a chance. I tried to help him see the message he was giving the others.

I used "news" as community building. I talked about myself, my family, my weekend. I had the kids do the same. We worked on learning how to listen to each other.

I had to help them learn how to work. Working together, talking together, my valuing their good working, all of us caring about each other. That's what community is.

I picked one academic thing to focus on—language literacy. To use words, to talk, to explain more deeply, to listen to and love literature.

When I started, I wanted to pack in as much academic learning as possible. It's hard to take it slow, to stop when things go wrong and talk about it. But you must. The academics really will get done! Kids learning how to work, how to take responsibility for their own learning and their own behaviors—*that* is building community. And it's worth the time it takes. They'll do unbelievably superb work once they get it—once they're a community.

With that hard group, we were not a community until January! This year it came so much faster.

What else? I wanted the kids to learn so much. And I thought I had to teach it all. I learned I didn't have to be everywhere at once, teaching, teaching. Kids could—and did—help each other. That's what I mean by community.

Learn to trust the kids. Let go of the control. Give them the materials. Build community. They can do really, really good work.

KRISTINE ANNUNZIATO

First grade, M.S. in Education, Hunter College, New York City, student teacher experience at CPE 1; five years of teaching experience in public school, two years in private school.

My first year I remember feeling petrified, doubtful about my practice. Did traditional teachers all around me know something I didn't know? Was I right about my practice? It was hard being the only learner-centered-classroom teacher in the whole school. Having support—from books, from courses, from former colleagues—was important.

When you're starting out, think about your day's schedule and what your options are. I tried to mimic my student teaching experience, but this didn't always work. I had to fit within the whole school schedule. Some things you have no choice about; you don't always have the luxury to re-create what you've learned. So if you have to teach reading at a certain time or from a certain basal, do it. You'll find time to put the good reading in. Be flexible.

Start out little by little. Sometimes, especially at first, don't give choices. Everyone gets the same project. They'll be learning how to use the materials correctly, how to share, take turns, keep voices down, help each other.

From whole-group projects you could move to two projects simultaneously. You could have math going—games that teach, manipulatives that teach largely without you, and writing, where some kids may be starting by drawing their story and you are available to write their words and sentences from their dictation.

As the group seems ready for more work on its own, think out which areas kids can work in most independently. Start by opening these first, and keep them all year so you are not trying to teach directly all things at the same time. Independent work can happen most easily in Legos™, blocks, dramatic play. You have little to teach about how to use these materials. These activities are "open ended"; there's not one right answer or concept to discover. Kids can use their imagination and investigate their own questions; they will usually be totally absorbed; they need you very little.

The listening area (books and tapes) is another area for independent work. Cooking, on the other hand, requires supervision. You may not be able to do it without help.

If your school permits, put a small table in the hall—to allow a couple of children to read or work there. Little kids love to read in the hall; it makes them feel so independent. It adds to their independence and to your space.

Second, use partnerships to free you up—and to teach children how to help and teach each other. Peer teaching works very well. Even very beginning readers can help each other—to interpret the pictures of the story, to supply a word that the partner may not know.

After you've thought about the organization of your daily schedule and the activities that you can have going simultaneously, think about the tone of your room. You want it to be quiet and productive all year long.

What are the routines and rules that will keep it so? Spend time helping the kids to know the rules and routines. I used to say, "What are we doing now? What happens next? Tell me."

Sometimes the room can feel chaotic. Look around. If it is, stop everything. Tell the kids what you're hearing/feeling. Give them a moment to be silent. Start over, or slow down.

If the school requirements are such that you have little time for wider-scoped activities and choices, you can still integrate some choice and active learning into the reading/writing periods. Puppets can go with a story or script; dioramas can illustrate a book.

Math, when you're not doing a whole-class lesson, can be active through the use of manipulatives; choice is built in where several materials can be used to discover or demonstrate a math concept.

Where you are allowed to have choice and active learning, pick activities that have meaning—that are not busy work or reward for the "real" work already done in reading and writing. Activities should be seen as an opportunity to learn more.

Have confidence that you will be able to "control" an active classroom. Kids love to learn this way, so teacher control as we usually think of it is not so much an issue. As you require children to be responsible learners, you also require them to be an integral part of the community you create in your classroom. They will be so thrilled to be the ones who help make decisions. They will want this community and will work for it.

KAREN CATHERS

Fourth grade, B.A., M.A., SUNY, New Paltz, NY. Six years of teaching "Life Positive" substance abuse prevention program, Ulster County, NY. Eleven years of teaching experience, New Paltz Central Schools. Member, Task Force for Change and Diversity, a community and school-based committee working on racism/sexism/homophobia in the schools.

What makes my classroom work is respect—and a sense of humor!

The first two weeks of school we spend an enormous amount of time on community building. It's intensive work. Respect for each other underlies community, and community is crucial to building a classroom in which kids have a lot of autonomy, in which academic learning happens.

I use a program called Project Charlie. Project Charlie is a highly structured program based on the belief that social skills are learnable skills, that people have choices about their behaviors, that they can learn to change them. Project Charlie is about communication—developing listening skills, expressing feelings, building friendship.

The first day we do name-learning activities: find someone in the classroom who has three pets, who has the same number of letters in their last name as you.

Then we interview each other and report to the class the results of the interview. We have a more personal view of each other this way.

All year long, when something happens that affects everybody, we stop. I say, "We need to talk about this." I also interrupt tattling. I ask, "What did you say to them about it?" I see myself as a mediator. It's not about finding fault. It's about finding solutions. There is not punishment. This approach makes kids more responsible for themselves and the classroom.

All year long we also do a weekly community meeting. Kids begin to trust it after awhile. When an issue comes up, they write it on the agenda;

they come to know that the meeting will solve the issue. The meeting has three steps: First, the class picks one of the listed issues to focus on. We do a whine-and-moan session, where kids describe the issue. After the description, I ask, "What solutions might we propose?" That's step 2. We write down all possible solutions and discuss these. We decide which ones we want to try. We want a consensus. We choose a solution. Step 3 is trying it out during the week, and discussing it as we use it. Is it working?

Generally, meetings deal with problems that involve many kids—like certain kids always get on the computer; maybe we're not getting to the bus on time.

Additionally, I use cooperative learning, which is also highly structured. I start with groups of two. Later, four kids make a group. A lot of time is spent setting it up and talking about how it went. Pointing out who helped the group and how we can make it happen better next time. One partner didn't study? Did the other not help? There is both an individual and a group grade for the work.

Kids get the feeling that they are truly respected, that this is a learning environment, that we are here to help each other.

I individualize and provide for autonomy within my curriculum. In spelling, kids pick the words from their own writing that they want to learn, groups of ten words at a time. They work with a partner to learn their own words and some of the partner's as well. They help their partner, and test each other.

In literature studies, children choose from three books for their silent reading and for their reading journal responses. For homework, they partner with people they would be willing to have help them. Again, they make the choices and take the responsibility.

We also do independent study. Kids choose to research any topic that interests them. They read for two weeks to learn about their subject (without taking notes) and then come up with a question within that subject that they want to research. Then they decide how to go about their research. Will they read about their topic, do an experiment? At the end, they make a presentation with a visual aid; they could make a poster or a model or write a play about their subject.

All through the year we discuss the process of learning. I ask each kid to ask himself, "What's important for me to learn—or am I wasting my time?"

The classroom is not always perfect. Sometimes you doubt yourself. But kids are so much fun. And they do have a real sense of what's right. I'm always impressed with their intelligence and sense of justice. It's really about listening to them, taking time to hear them. It's about supporting the making of choices, taking individual responsibility and responsibility for making the community work.

APPENDIX A

Setting Up the Classroom

∽

Kristine Annunziato

SETTING UP FOR LOWER GRADES

Setting up the classroom in September takes a lot of time. The better organized you are the more you help promote student autonomy. An early childhood classroom should have many different areas. The size of your room will affect how many areas you are able to have and how many children may work in an area. Remember to begin simply and add to each area as the students become more familiar with their environment. I have composed a list of suggested areas and materials for an early childhood classroom.

Classroom Library

An early childhood class library is best organized by categorizing the books in bins. The bins should be labeled. Sometimes teachers color-code them in order to keep the categories together. The bins should not have too many books so that selection is easy. Books may be organized by genre, author, or subject. Some of the bins may include books by Leo Lionni, Dr. Seuss, Vera B. Williams, Eric Carle; Poetry; Nonfiction; Frog and Toad Books; Sunshine Books; Amelia Bedelia books. Other categories are: books about dinosaurs, about animals, Magic School Bus, Foretells and Fables, Biographies, Chapter Books, Little Bear Books, Story Box Books, and Nate the Great Books.

Some teachers discuss categories with their class before setting up the library in the beginning of the year. This allows for group decision making about what they think is important and how they think it should be organized. It is also a good idea to start off small and add to the library as the children become more familiar with the routines. Then add bins of books over the course of the year, taking into account the children's suggestions.

Writing Area

Storage materials include shallow bins from the hardware store, cans of different sizes covered in colored contact paper.

Labeling each bin and its contents helps keep things orderly.

Materials include pencils (plenty), colored pencils, Cray-Pas®, markers (thick and thin), staplers, tape, glue (Elmer's™ and glue sticks), an assortment of paper (in small quantities), scissors, writing journals, bins for "work in progress" and "finished work," file folders for completed work.

Math Area

Provide:

books about numbers, math journals, pattern blocks, attribute blocks, unifix cubes, Cuisinaire rods™ (essential), dice, rulers (inches on one side, centimeters on the other). Include a few 18-inch rulers, and a couple of yard/meter sticks, tape measures, small clocks, tangrams, color tiles.

counting and sorting materials: beans, buttons, beads, and colored pasta.

math games: bingo; connect four; dominoes; playing cards with kings, queens, jacks removed; and teacher-made counting, adding and subtracting games.

Science Area

Provide:

animals: ideally, have lots of them after awhile, not all at once in September; guinea pigs, fish, snakes, iguanas, hermit crabs, land snails, meal worms.

journals: science journals or paper for noting observations (I sometimes have a standard form including name, date, "my observation," and a space to draw a picture).

magnets: along with magnetic and nonmagnetic materials, magnifying glasses.

found items: a bin with interesting objects that children can add to over the course of the year.

Once again, I cannot stress enough the fact that you would not have all these materials out at once. They should reflect your curriculum and allow for children to observe and document their discoveries over the course of the year.

Blocks

Blocks should be placed neatly on shelves and labeled according to size and shape. I cut out an exact size of the block as a label and attach it to the shelf.

Provide:

a bin with wooden people

a bin with vehicles

a bin with different signs (the children can make these)

an area for large index cards so children can label their block structures

Before setting up blocks, take time to think about putting them away from quiet places since their use tends to be somewhat noisy.

Art/Construction Area

Provide:

paints (tempera, watercolors) and paintbrushes (different sizes)

construction paper, different size drawing paper, oak tag, markers, crayons, Cray-Pas®

collage materials (these materials can be collected). Some useful things are colored pasta, different colored shapes cut from construction paper, beans, ribbons, wrapping paper

good junk: this would include boxes of different sizes; Styrofoam™ for packing; egg cartons; paper plates; cardboard scraps; natural objects such as shells, wood, rocks; and any interesting objects which can be transformed into an artistic object (for "good junk" I usually send home a letter asking for donations)

woodworking supplies: wood scraps, hammer, nails, screws, small saw, clamp/or table w/vise, mitre box, screwdriver, pliers

Listening Area

Provide:

books with their recordings on cassette tape (Scholastic Book orders are a great way to begin this collection.)

tape recorder with two to four headphones (You need to get an attachment to allow for several headphones.)

Some teachers choose books and record their own voices onto cassettes.

Cooking Area *(large enough for two to four children)*

Provide: small, medium, and large mixing bowls; measuring cups; measuring spoons; small, medium, and large spoons and spatulas; cookie trays for baking; muffin trays (miniature trays bake twenty-four); pie plates; rolling pins; cookie cutters; table top oven; hot pads; aprons

Dramatic Play *(enough space for three to four children)*

Provide: small table and chairs, play dishes, cups, pots, telephone, container or rack for dress-up clothes, male and female doll babies (various races)

You may add or subtract: suitcase, doll buggy, firefighter and police officer hats.

Sand Table *(up to four children)*

Provide: dry sand first (add water for wet sand later); scoops, containers of different sizes and shapes, strainers (put these in wet sand also), cookie tins (put these in dry sand also), water wheel, funnels

Water Table *(up to 4 children)*

Same as for sand table. You may add or subtract: turkey baster, water pump, and plastic tubing of different diameters

Other Areas to Consider

Games, puzzles, Legos™

SETTING UP FOR UPPER GRADES

Upper-grade classrooms may not be able to have separate areas for work in science, art, and dramatics. Given that upper-grade rooms may be smaller than those of early childhood and that children's bodies are bigger, work tends to be spread over the entire room. Activities involving each of the subject areas may go on simultaneously side by side. Materials, however, are likely to be kept where they most logically seem to fit—that is, science stuff is kept together, math stuff has its place, art its place, and so on.

The science, math, and art materials are often those of the lower grades (paints, junk cardboard and boxes, magnifiers and magnets, Legos™) plus materials that require greater skill to use, such as foam board, X-Acto™ blades, microscopes, computers. Math games can be made to dovetail with the appropriate curriculum.

SCROUNGING FOR SUPPLIES

At the beginning of the year, send home a letter asking for the cardboard boxes, paper towel rolls, empty oatmeal containers, and other junk you need for construction. Ask for buttons, spools, and fabric scraps. If your school does not have plentiful supplies, ask for pencils, crayons, and markers. Be sure to say these are for use by the class as a whole. Parents can sometimes supply an armchair, a rug. Someone may be able to donate an old but usable refrigerator

A rug cleaner may provide a rug that a customer has failed to pick up. A wallpaper store may provide old wallpaper sample books, good for making covers for kids' writing when glued to shirt cardboard. A hardware store may contribute nails, screws, wire, washers; an art store, foam board scraps; a lumber yard, wood scraps.

Make the math games. Save your money for the Cuisinaire™ rods and pattern blocks you can't make. Ask a lumber yard to cut you five-ply wood to make geoboards. Use brass nails with knob heads for these. Cuisinaire™ "flats" can be made with three-ply wood and can be painted orange to match the rods.

Room Layouts

Hettie Jordan-Villanova

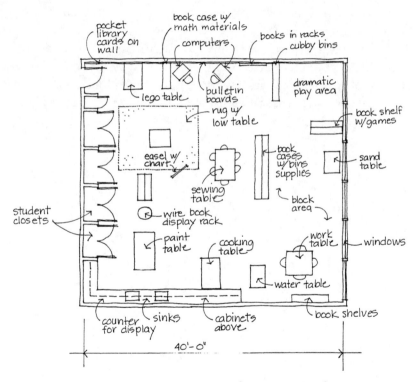

Figure B-1 Room Layout for Lower Grades

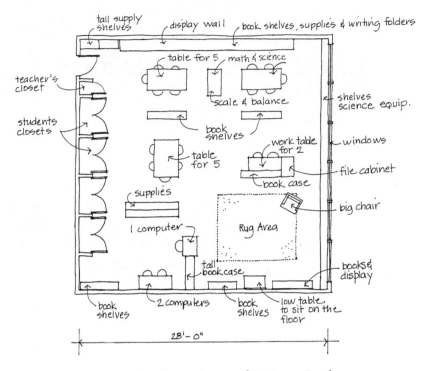

Figure B-2 Room Layout for Upper Grades

APPENDIX C

Sample Organization of the Day, Third/Fourth-Grade Room

⟳

8:45 A.M.	Children arrive, turn in homework, chat quietly with each other. Teacher talks with kids, listening to important news, assessing who may need support to start the day comfortably.
9:00 A.M.	Lights off signal. Children come to meeting area.
	Meeting agenda includes announcements, may include a minilesson, discussion of a newspaper article, important classroom issue. Teacher checks to see that each child knows what his or her project work is and dismisses to projects, a few children at a time.
	When routines are firm and projects last more than one day, this meeting may be omitted. Teacher stops children at the door to be sure each knows what his work is that morning.
9:20 A.M.	Project time.
10:35 A.M.	Five-minute warning. Then clean up and return to meeting area.
10:50 A.M.	Sharing-time meeting: A group or two describes its work, questions, discussion.
11:05 A.M.	Quiet reading.
11:50 A.M.	Books away. Pencils counted. Dismissal for lunch, recess.
12:45 P.M.	Math.
1:30 P.M.	Writing workshop.
2:15 P.M.	Return to meeting area for teacher read-aloud. Pencils counted.
2:50 P.M.	Coats on for 3:00 P.M. dismissal.

APPENDIX D

Recognizing Learnings in an Activity-Oriented Classroom

∞

AN OBSERVATIONAL FORM

Teaching (and lesson plans) need to begin with the child. A good way to start might be to observe what children actually do with the materials and areas set up in the classroom. Watch what they do, listen to what they say. Write it down, as verbatim as you can. Then look at your observations. What learnings, if any, do you think you see?

Area: _____ (library, math area, writing area, dramatic play, blocks, cooking, sand, water)

POSSIBLE LEARNINGS

Academic	*Social*	*Affective*

Appendix E

Lesson Plan for an Individual Child

∞

Tracy Kramer

Background

I have observed that Allissa has trouble focusing on her working during writing workshop. She often spends an entire session coloring one picture, but she is not concentrating on the drawing. Rather, the way she draws indicates that her mind is elsewhere. For example, she creates a pattern and then repeats it endlessly all over the page, or colors a simple shape over and over with a crayon. She only wants to write make-believe stories. These are usually made up of a series of happy images, like a girl picking flowers.

Overall Goals

I would like Allissa to explore other types of writing. Perhaps she could write a biography of someone she knows or a book about the Dominican Republic, where her beloved Papi is from. I would like her to choose a theme for her book and stick with it for the whole book.

Day 1 (11/7/94)

Objective: I would like Allissa to begin work on a short book (two to four pages) about a real subject.

Implementation: When I approached Allissa, she was working on a book that was made up of a series of seemingly unrelated images: a girl picking flowers, a pool, a penguin. When I asked what the book was about, she answered, "penguins." We titled the book "Things I Like" and moved on to a new book. This time, she insisted that she wanted to write about me. She was going to make me picking flowers and me dressing up in pretty clothes and looking in the mirror.

Assessment: Allissa did not seem interested in writing a book. She answered me with one-word responses. When I asked her what she wanted to write about next, she responded, without hesitation, "You." It seemed that she was picking the most obvious subject without putting any thought into the matter. Her eyes wandered around the room while I was talking to her.

DAY 2 (11/15/94)

Objective: I am hoping to get Allissa to finish up her pretend-story about me. I would like to encourage her to write a real story, perhaps a biography of someone. I would also like to help her build some of the mechanical skills of writing.

Implementation: Allissa told me that she lost the story about me. She was working on a "dream book" with a pool. The writing book was opening the wrong way. I got a few real books, and we discovered together that they all open the same way. I suggested that she number her pages beginning with "the real number one," which she did enthusiastically. She wrote each number backward. She chose a subject for each page that is related to the title of the book, "My Dream Book." One of the wishes was "No fighting." I asked her about this, and her curt, uninterested answers turned into a flow of impassioned words. She told me that she wishes her parents would stop all the fighting, and she described several incidents in which fights erupted and how she felt.

Assessment: It seems like the unrest at home is on her mind a lot. This could very likely be one of the reasons she is often so distracted.

DAY 3 (11/17/94)

Objective: To get Allissa to write something that is really important to her.

Implementation: I told Allissa that many parents fight, even mine, and I hate it when mine fight, too. She seemed surprised by this information. I told her that it might make me feel better to read a book about someone else who was going through the same thing as I was, maybe feeling some of the same feelings. She asked if it could be a "private book" that no one would see but us. I said, "Of course," and the words flowed! She finally had lots to write about. I noticed that she was tripping over her mechanical writing skills (she doesn't have some of the sound-symbol relationships), so we alternated doing the actual writing. I took dictation, and gave her the pencil when it came to a word I knew she could do. Her pictures were more detailed than any I have seen her do in the past. The harsh lines and brown, black, and gray tones really conveyed her feelings.

Assessment: Allissa does have a lot to say. She was very intent on her work today. Her eyes did not wander around the room at all. Hopefully, this book will help build the confidence she needs and, when she finishes, she can apply what she has learned to writing other books and materials. Allissa has trouble with letters. She frequently writes letters and numbers backward. Even when she is copying a letter from the alphabet in her folder, she sometimes writes the wrong letter. Right now, I am primarily concerned with the content aspect of her work, since she is working on the mechanical skills with one specialist in school and another several days a week after school. I would like to continue to help her discover subjects she is interested in and that she feels a need to write about.

Model Making at CPE*

∽

Deborah Meier

One of the activities that goes on in every CPE class is the ever-present constructing of models: models of houses, skyscrapers, bridges, towns, cars, people, animals, robots, spaceships, and odd imaginary objects. Why? Do you sometimes wonder?

Of course, children love to make models; it's fun. But in fact we don't decide what to do just because it's "fun." Sometimes it's a clue to us, as educators; activities that really engross kids, that they "fall in love with," are likely to be powerful learning tools. But we have our own reasons too for encouraging, not just putting up with, all that building of models.

In the process of building a model, lots of important questions naturally arise. You have to look closely, read carefully, and think: Where do the eyes actually go? What shape are they? How are the legs connected to the body? Which is bigger? What enables the wheels to turn? How many windows and doors are needed? What are all those "things" on the roofs of buildings? Each of these questions raises even more questions about biology, mechanics, physics, and social studies. Each question leads us back to researching and observing even more thoughtfully.

Models also always involve scale because they are rarely life-size. As soon as we reduce the size, we're into a lot of interesting questions and calculations. We're at the heart of mathematics: What happens if we make something half as big? Half what? A half of a glass of water actually could have two different meanings, although conventionally we know what's being asked for. If every aspect of that glass were halved, it would contain a fourth as much water if we made it half as wide and half as tall! We're swiftly into the whole realm of comparisons and relationships, which is what math and science are all about.

---

* Originally published in *Central Park East News*, a weekly newsletter to parents.

A model is also an experience a child has gone through in a way that requires him or her to put a lot of things together; it's a way of acting on an idea using a wide array of knowledge and skill. It builds a sense of power and confidence. It provides a chance to use new skills—measuring, drawing, using a ruler or straight edge, finding an angle, using scissors or saws and hammers.

Finally, models bring the subject matter itself to life for children and thus create the possibility for a permanent love affair between the wonders of the world and a child's natural curiosity. That's not a trivial function of education. Enthusiasm for learning is at the heart of being well educated.

APPENDIX G

A Sample Web:
A Curriculum Planning Device

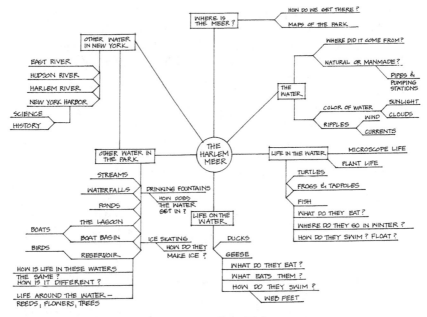

Figure G-1 Web

End Notes

∽

1. For a highly readable description of the school, see David Bensman (1987), *Quality Education in the Inner City: The Story of the Central Park East Schools* (New York: Desktop Publishing by Kramer Communications). Copies available from Central Park East 1, 1531 Madison Ave., New York, NY 10029.

2. Howard Gardner (1978), *Frames of Mind—The Theory of Multiple Intelligences* (New York: Basic Books). Gardner proposes these categories of intelligences: linguistic, musical, logical-mathematical, spatial, bodily-kinesthetic, intra- and interpersonal.

3. John Dewey (1902), *The Child and the Curriculum* and *The School and Society*. (Chicago: University of Chicago Press) includes examples of using hands-on activities to expand and deepen knowledge; and William Crain (1992), *Theories of Development, Concepts and Applications*, 3rd ed. (Englewood Cliffs, NJ: Prentice-Hall).

4. For studies of one such school—Central Park East 1 in New York City—see: David Bensman (1994), *Lives of the Graduates of Central Park East Elementary School: Where Have They Gone? What Did They Really Learn?* (New York: NCREST, Teachers College, Columbia University), and Jon Snyder, Ann Lieberman, Maritza B. MacDonald, and A. Lin Goodwin (1992), *Makers of Meaning in a Learning-Centered School: A Case Study of Central Park East Elementary School* (New York: NCREST, Teachers College, Columbia University).

5. Mary Barr, Dana Craig, Donna Fisette, and Margaret Syverson (1999), *Assessing Literacy with the Learning Record* (Portsmouth, NH: Heinemann Educational Books).

6. Lillian Weber (November 1973), "But Is It Science?" *Science in the Open Classroom* (New York: The Workshop Center, The City College of New York).

7. Educators for Social Responsibility, 23 Garden Street, Cambridge, MA 02138.

8. Eleanor Duckworth (1996), *The Having of Wonderful Ideas and Other Essays on Teaching and Learning* (New York: Teachers College Press).

9. David Macaulay, (1975), *Pyramid* (Boston: Hougton Mifflin), (1976, *Underground* (Boston: Houghton Mifflin), (1977), *Castle* (Boston: Houghton Mifflin).

10. David Hawkins (February 1965), "Messing About in Science," *Science and Children* (Arlington, VA: National Science Teachers Association), and (Summer 1965), "On Living in Trees," *Colorado Quarterly*.

Suggested Readings

Charney, Ruth Sidney. 1991. *Teaching Children to Care: Management in the Responsive Classroom.* Greenfield, MA: Northeast Foundation for Children.

An excellent description of how to organize the classroom community. Discusses the role of choice in helping kids learn to make good decisions; discipline and how to teach it.

Cohen, Dorothy H. 1972. *The Learning Child.* New York: Schocken Books.

An eminently readable and comprehensive account of the ways children learn at the different stages of their growth. The child at five, at six and seven, and at eight to eleven is examined, and the factors are described that educators need to take into account to make their teaching appropriate. Children make sense of their world through active and concrete participation in it, even in the eight to eleven category, although at this age more abstract thinking is possible. Work in blocks, clay, and construction materials is important in helping the child move from concrete to symbolic learning. Considers the heavy push for early reading instruction as inappropriate and damaging. Traditional education with its focus on externally imposed curricula, uniform standards, and tests is seen as damaging to the child's curiosity, initiative, and ability to grow intellectually.

Devries Rheta, and Kohlberg, Lawrence. 1990. *Constructivist Early Education: Overview and Comparison with Other Programs.* Washington, D.C.: National Association for the Education of Young Children.

Describes "constructivist education," its roots in the philosophy of Jean Piaget, current practices, and research needed for the future. Chapters on reading, writing, math; excellent and quite specific description of teacher's role. Lots of information, densely packed. Not an easy read, but a detailed, thorough exposition.

Dewey, John. 1966. *Democracy and Education.* New York: The Free Press.

Dewey's theory of education. Maintains that a democratic society must allow for intellectual freedom and the diverse gifts of members; discusses how to develop the kind of education appropriate to the development of a democracy.

Grennon, Jacqueline. 1993. *In Search of Understanding: The Case for Constructivist Classrooms.* Alexandria, VA.: Association for Supervision and Curriculum Development.

A rationale for progressive education in the 1990s based on new research and data.

Harlen, Wynne. 1996. *The Teaching of Science in Primary Schools,* 2nd ed. London: David Fulton.

Describes the "interactive" science teacher's role in the development of children's ideas and process skills. Includes questions that teachers can ask to foster inquiry learning, suggestions for assessment of process skills, and more.

Himley, Margaret, ed. 1999. *Prospect Starting-Up Stories: The Descriptive Review of the Child.* New York: Teachers College Press.

A process developed initially at the Prospect School in Vermont helps teachers examine how particular children function in the classroom. "The descriptive review" looks at the child in terms of physical presence and gesture, disposition and temperament, connections with other people, strong interests and preferences, and role as thinker and learner. The review is done by a group of teachers, with the child's teacher presenting. (This book is comprised of actual transcriptions of teacher reviews.)

Hirsch, Elisabeth S., ed. 1996. *The Block Book,* 3rd ed. Washington, DC: National Association for the Education of Young Children.

A must for every teacher. Discusses the role of block building for furthering cognitive growth. Blocks are examined for their role in physical development, mathematics, science, art, language arts, social studies, social-emotional growth. Lavishly illustrated with drawings and photos of children's work.

Loughlin, Catherine L., and Guina, Joseph. 1982. The Learning Environment: An Instructional Strategy. New York: Teachers College Press.

Discussion and illustrations of room layouts, guides for deciding what materials to provide. Especially useful chapter on provisioning for children with special needs.

Meier, Deborah. 1995. *The Power of Their Ideas.* Boston: Beacon Press.

Description and discussion of the small schools' movement, the organization of the Central Park East elementary schools and the high school and the meaning of these experiences for our thinking about effective schools and public policy.

Mitchell, Lucy Sprague. 1991. *Young Geographers,* 4th ed. New York: Bank Street College of Education.

Geography described as the study of relationships between humankind and the environment. It is the relationship to people that makes the facts of geography meaningful. Describes in readable, usable detail the development of geography studies from kindergarten through the class of twelve-year-olds. The kindergarten starts with trips to study the neighborhood; the classroom provides the experience of re-creating the neighborhood through block building, drawing, and dramatic play. Flat maps, relief maps and globes are created as children mature. The stages of development and teacher interventions are described. Includes an appendix listing sources for map-making supplies. A superb book for an "alive" geography curriculum.

Pratt, Caroline. 1990. *I Learn from Children.* New York: First Perennial Library Edition, Harper and Row.

One of the country's first practitioners of progressive education, the designer of the blocks now widely used in early education describes her own evolution from a traditional teacher in a one-room schoolhouse to an innovative thinker and teacher. Watching children at play, she came to believe that play is children's work. From this understanding of the child's need to explore the world and to re-create it through play, she founded, first in a borrowed room, then in a building of its own , the school that became City and Country School. The use of real-world experiences, and the classroom activities that follow, and the organization through the grades are described. A fascinating read.

Rogovin, Paula. 1998. *Classroom Interviews: A World of Learning.* Portsmith, NH: Heinemann.

Describes an integrated social studies curriculum on the themes of family and work. Uses interviews by the children of parents and others as the beginning source of information. Shows how to enlarge the initial learning and how to integrate the information with reading, writing, art, music, geography, history. Designed as a first-grade curriculum but could be easily adapted for other grades. A definitely doable and important curriculum.

Index